EXPERIMENTS FOR FUTURE
PHYSICISTS

ROBERT GARDNER
AND JOSHUA CONKLIN

Enslow Publishing
101 W. 23rd Street
Suite 240
New York, NY 10011
USA

enslow.com

Published in 2017 by Enslow Publishing, LLC.
101 W. 23rd Street, Suite 240, New York, NY 10011

Library of Congress Cataloging-in-Publication Data

Names: Gardner, Robert, 1929- author. | Conklin, Joshua, author.
Title: Experiments for future physicists / Robert Gardner and Joshua Conklin.
Description: New York, NY : Enslow Publishing, LLC, 2017 | Series: Experiments for future STEM
  professionals | Includes bibliographical references and index.
Identifiers: LCCN 2016009260| ISBN 9780766078550 (library bound)
Subjects: LCSH: Physics—Experiments—Juvenile literature.
Classification: LCC QC33 .G368 2017 | DDC 530.078—dc23
LC record available at http://lccn.loc.gov/2016009260

Printed in the United States of America

To Our Readers: We have done our best to make sure all website addresses in this book were active and appropriate when we went to press. However, the author and the publisher have no control over and assume no liability for the material available on those websites or on any websites they may link to. Any comments or suggestions can be sent by e-mail to customerservice@enslow.com.

Photos Credits: Cover, James Whitaker/DigitalVision/Getty Images (physicist), imagenavi/Getty Images (lab background throughout book), Titov Nikolai/Shutterstock.com (atom symbol), elic/Shutterstock.com (red geometric background throughout book), Zffoto/Shutterstock.com (white textured background throughout book).

Illustrations by Joseph Hill.

CONTENTS

INTRODUCTION

Physics is the study of the properties of matter and energy and their relationship to one another. People who study physics ask such questions as: What are the basic particles of matter? What was the origin of the universe? How is the universe changing and how might it change in the future?

While physics can be used to study some of the universe's great mysteries, it also deals with practical problems. It can be used to study sustainable forms of energy, such as nuclear fusion and fission. It involves designing and developing better ways to use radiation to treat cancer, improve computers and computer games, and develop better medical and information technology. The practical applications of physics are virtually endless.

TO BECOME A PHYSICIST

Physicists are intelligent, imaginative, and creative. They can work independently, and they enjoy solving problems. If you have similar traits, you would probably enjoy a career as a physicist.

To prepare for such a career, you should begin in high school. Take as many mathematics and science courses as possible. Take English and other subjects that challenge you to think in different ways. Read lots of books about physics and physicists. Reading biographies of some of the great physicists—Galileo, Huygens, Newton, Boyle, Volta, Faraday, Dalton, Thomson, Maxwell, Einstein, Bohr—will provide insight into the nature of physics, scientific inquiry, and the joy of discovery.

To gain admission to a great college, strive for good grades, do well on the SATs, and develop interesting and challenging physics projects for science fairs. You might also consider summer camps dedicated to science or internships in scientific fields. By doing so, you will have information that will help convince admissions officers that you are a good candidate.

As a college freshman, you should enroll in physics and calculus. The physics course might be quite difficult. Some colleges make the course challenging to "weed out" less dedicated students. If you really want to pursue physics, hang in there. Later courses will probably not prove as difficult. In your second year, you should probably take intermediate mechanics, electromagnetic theory, and more calculus. As a junior, you can select from a variety of courses including optics, thermodynamics, atomic and nuclear theory, and statistical mechanics. In your senior year, you will probably take quantum mechanics and some other courses you didn't select the year before.

With a BS (Bachelor of Science) in physics, you could probably find a job in the industry. However, you may find it more rewarding to continue your education and open up new avenues for your career. If you would like to teach physics, spend a year or two in graduate school taking courses in both physics and education on your way to a master's degree. That degree would qualify you to teach physics at the high school or community college level.

If you are interested in doing research and teaching in a college or university, you should obtain a PhD in physics. This will require four to five years of coursework and research. You will probably work with a professor as a research assistant. It will also involve publishing some original research, but your advising professor can suggest research that will lead to publishable findings.

Once you have your PhD, you can find work in government, industry, or academics. If you choose the academic path, you'll have more freedom to do research of your own choosing.

WHAT DO PHYSICISTS DO?

Given that they tackle questions about both the universe and the practical problems of industry, physicists work in a huge variety of fields. Some focus on theory, exploring the basic ideas about the structure of matter, the generation and transmission of energy, the origin of the universe, and the Big Bang. Many physicists work in astronomy investigating black holes, the origin of matter, and the size of the universe. Others seek answers to practical problems involving computers, medical technology, engineering research, meteorology, and even financial analysis.

All physicists work to solve problems or answer questions. Those who work in academic fields are often free to pursue problems that interest them the most.

A recent search of job opportunities for physicists returned a slew of results. A few of the industries and schools seeking physicists included work in radiation therapy, teaching physics at the college level, space research, calibrating and testing a variety of machines, journalism, high energy theory, hardware and software development, biomedical imaging, nuclear research, fiber optics, developing computer models in mathematics and science, and so on. Should you work hard to become a physicist, there will be multiple career paths.

THE SCIENTIFIC METHOD

Many physicists are involved in scientific research seeking answers to the problems they strive to understand. They ask questions, make careful observations, and conduct research. Different areas of physics use different approaches. Depending on the problem, one method is likely to be better than another. Designing a new spaceship, finding a safer way to use radiation in medicine, or searching for dark matter, require different techniques, but they all demand an understanding of how science is conducted.

Despite the differences, all scientists use a similar general approach while experimenting called the scientific method. In most experiments, some or all of the following steps are used: making an observation, formulating a question, making a hypothesis (one possible answer to the question) and a prediction (an if-then statement), designing and conducting one or more experiments, analyzing the results in order to reach conclusions about the prediction, and the acceptance or rejection of the hypothesis. Scientists share their findings. They write articles about their experiments and results. Their writings are reviewed by other scientists before being published in journals for wider circulation.

You might wonder how to start an experiment. When you observe something in the world, your curiosity may spark a question. Your question, which could arise from an earlier experiment or from reading, may be answered by a well-designed investigation. Once you have a question, you can make a hypothesis. Your hypothesis is a possible answer to the question (what you think will happen). Once you have a hypothesis, it is time to design an experiment to test a consequence of your hypothesis.

In most cases, it is appropriate to do a controlled experiment. This means having two groups that are treated exactly the same except for the single factor being tested. That factor is called a *variable*. For example, suppose your question is: "Is the intensity of light inversely proportional to the distance from the light source?"

You would use a single light source placed in total darkness. You would then measure the intensity of the light at varying distances. Your results might look something like those in Table 1.

Table 1: The intensity of light at known distances from a light source.

Distance from light (m)	Intensity of light (foot-candles)	1/d²
1.0	20.0	1.0
2.0	5.0	0.25
3.0	2.2	0.11
4.0	1.3	0.063

The data shows that your hypothesis is not correct. Doubling the distance did not half the light's intensity. Doubling the distance reduced the intensity to one-fourth. This indicates that the intensity is inversely proportional to the distance squared. Plotting a graph of light intensity vs 1/distance² would result in the graph shown in Figure 1.

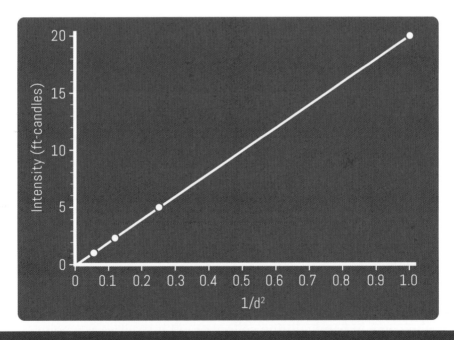

Figure 1. A graph shows light intensity versus the inverse square of the distance from the light source. The graph indicates that light intensity is inversely proportional to the square of the distance from the light source.

You would conclude that your original hypothesis was not correct. But you would also conclude that the data shows that light intensity is inversely proportional to the square of the distance from the light source.

You would probably repeat the experiment and collect more data to confirm your conclusion.

Two other terms are often used in scientific experiments—*dependent* and *independent variables*. The dependent variable depends on the value of the independent variable. For example, the intensity of the light in the experiment above is the dependent variable. It depends on the distance from the light. The distance is the independent variable.

BEFORE YOU BEGIN EXPERIMENTING

At times, as you do the experiments and other activities in this book, you may need the help of a partner. It would be most enjoyable to work with someone who also loves to experiment. **If safety issues or danger are involved in doing an experiment, you will be warned. In some cases, to avoid danger, you will be asked to work with an adult. Please do so**. Don't take any chances that could lead to an injury.

Like any good scientist, you will find it useful to record your ideas, notes, data, and conclusions in a notebook. By doing so, you can keep track of the information you gather and the conclusions you reach. It will allow you to refer to things you have done and help you in doing future projects. It may also come in handy during college or job interviews as a point of reference.

SAFETY FIRST

Safety is important in science and engineering. Certain rules apply when you are conducting experiments. Some of the rules below may seem obvious to you and others may not, but it is important that you follow all of them.

1. Have an adult help you whenever this book, or any other, so advises.
2. Wear eye protection and closed-toe shoes (not sandals). Tie back long hair.
3. Do not eat or drink while experimenting. Never taste substances being used (unless instructed to do so).
4. Do not touch chemicals with your bare hands. Use tools, such as spatulas, to transfer chemicals from place to place.
5. The liquid in some thermometers is mercury (a dense liquid metal). It is dangerous to touch mercury or breathe mercury vapor. Mercury thermometers have been banned in many states. When doing experiments that require you to measure temperature, use only electronic or non-mercury thermometers, such as those filled with alcohol. If you have a mercury thermometer in the house, **ask an adult** if it can be taken to a local thermometer exchange location.
6. Do only those experiments that are described in this book or those that have been approved by **an adult**.
7. Maintain a serious attitude while conducting experiments. Never engage in horseplay or practical jokes.
8. Before beginning an experiment, read all the instructions carefully and be sure you understand them.

9. Remove all items not needed for the experiment from your work space.
10. At the end of every activity, clean all materials used and put them away. Then wash your hands thoroughly with soap and water.

The chapters that follow contain experiments and information that every future young physicist should know. They will also help you to decide if being a physicist is a career you would like to pursue.

CHAPTER ONE

KINEMATICS

Kinematics is the study of motion without considering its causes. It provides an understanding of the meaning and measurement of speed, velocity, acceleration, and vectors. Let's get started.

EXPERIMENT 1

SPEED AND VELOCITY

To measure speed, you'll need to measure a distance and a time. It can be done by simply taking a walk while wearing a watch.

1. Walk the length of a football field from end line to end line (360 feet). At the start of

THINGS YOU WILL NEED

- **football field or any reasonable known walkable length**
- **stopwatch, phone, or watch that can measure seconds**

your walk, start a stopwatch or phone timer, or note the time on a watch that can measure seconds.
2. Walk at a steady pace. When you reach the other end line, stop the stopwatch or note the time on the watch.
3. Record the time it took you to walk 360 feet or whatever distance you walked.
4. Using the data (time and distance), calculate your average speed.

If it took you 90 seconds to walk 360 feet, your average speed was:
$$\text{speed} = \frac{360 \text{ ft}}{90 \text{ s}} = 4.0 \text{ ft/s}.$$

5. Repeat the experiment, but this time run the same distance. What was your speed when you ran the distance?

To find your velocity, you need to know the direction you walked. *Velocity* is speed in a particular direction. So if you walked 360 feet North in 100 seconds, your velocity was 3.6 ft/s North.

VECTORS

Velocities and any measurement that has a direction as well as a magnitude (size) can be represented by vectors. Vectors are arrows. The length of a velocity vector represents speed.

The velocity's direction is given by the way the arrow points. For example, a velocity of 6.0 ft/s could be represented by an arrow 3.0 cm long that points north. On maps, as you know, North is toward the top, South is toward the bottom, East is to the right, and West is to the left.

The vector for 6.0 ft/s North is shown in Figure 2a. Other parts of Figure 2 show displacement vectors as well as velocity vectors. Displacement vectors represent a length and a direction.

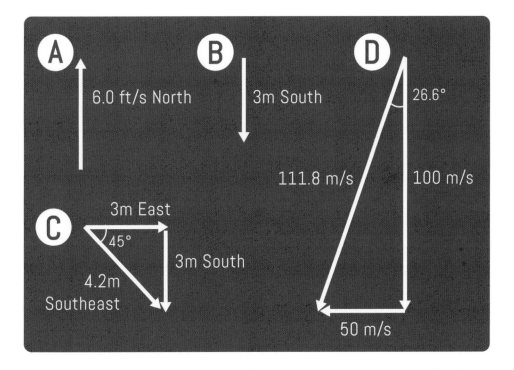

Figure 2. a) A velocity vector representing 6.0 ft/s North. b) A displacement vector representing 3 meters South. c) The sum of a displacement vector 3 meters East + a displacement vector 3 meters South is the hypotenuse—a displacement vector of 4.2 meters Southeast. d) The drawing shows the vector sum of an airplane velocity of 100 m/s South in a West wind of 50 m/s, which gives the plane a velocity of 111.8 m/s at 26.6° West of South.

All vectors of the same type can be added and subtracted in a geometrical fashion as shown in Figure 2c and 2d.

ACCELERATION

When you get into a car or a bus, the vehicle is at rest, with speed and velocity at zero. Once moving, it speeds up until it reaches a final cruising speed. The increase in speed occurs because the driver steps on the accelerator. The accelerator is so named because, you guessed it, it causes the vehicle to accelerate; that is, it causes the vehicle to change its speed and velocity.

Acceleration is defined as the change in velocity divided by the change in time (the time for the change in velocity to occur.) In mathematical terms:

$a = \Delta v / \Delta t$ where a is acceleration, v is velocity, t is time, and Δ (delta) means change in. So acceleration is equal to a change in velocity divided by the change in time required for velocity change to take place.

Suppose a vehicle that was at rest reaches a cruising speed of 60 kilometers/hour (km/h), or 16.7 m/s, after 60 seconds (1.0 minute). Its average acceleration was:

$$a = \Delta v / \Delta t = \frac{60 \text{ km/h}}{60 \text{ s}} = 1 \text{ km/h/s}$$

or $a = \dfrac{16.7 \text{m/s}}{1.0 \text{ min}} = 16.7 \text{ m/s/min.}$

EXPERIMENT 2

BUILDING AN ACCELEROMETER

The accelerometers you can build will indicate acceleration and show the direction of the acceleration. More expensive accelerometers can give both direction and magnitude. You can build two different accelerometers. Then, in Experiment 3, you will use them to detect accelerations and their directions. Some of the results may surprise you.

THINGS YOU WILL NEED

- **thread**
- **T-pin or large needle**
- **tape**
- **clear plastic jar with screw-on cap**
- **cork or other light material such as Styrofoam**
- **vial or test tube and cork to fit opening**
- **small piece of soap**

1. Insert a T-pin or large needle into a cork or a piece of Styrofoam. (See Figure 3a).
2. Tie one end of a length of thread to the T-pin. Tape the other end of the thread securely to the screw-on cap of a clear plastic jar (Figure 3a). Make sure the thread is not so long that the cork will rub against the bottom of the jar when the assembled accelerometer is inverted (Figure 3b).

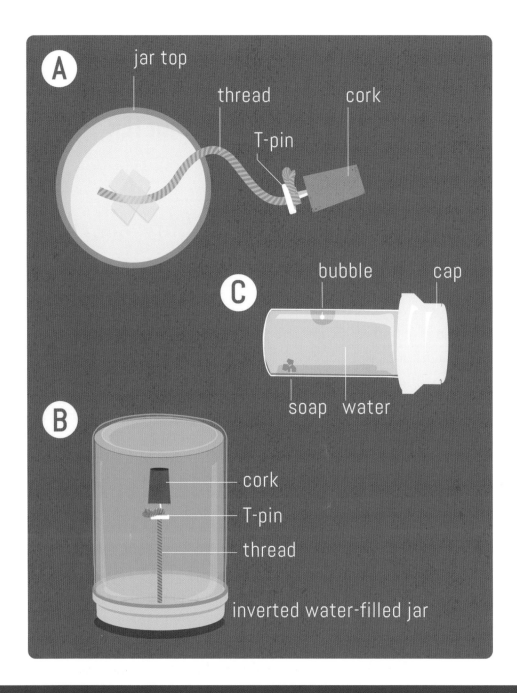

Figure 3. Two accelerometers you can build are shown here. a) The cap assembly for the jar accelerometer. b) The assembled jar accelerometer. c) A vial or test tube accelerometer uses a bubble to indicate acceleration.

3. Fill the jar with water, screw on the cap assembly, and invert the jar.

4. You can also make a vial or test tube accelerometer. Fill the vial or tube with water leaving just enough space for a small bubble of air. Add a tiny piece of soap. The soap will prevent the bubble from sticking to the vial's surface. Cap the vial, or cork the test tube, and lay it on its side (Figure 3c).

EXPERIMENT 3

TESTING THE ACCELEROMETERS

Now that you have built the accelerometers, you can test them to see how they indicate acceleration.

1. Place both accelerometers on a level table or counter.

2. Pull each one so that it accelerates. Notice that the cork or bubble always moves in the direction of the acceleration, which is also the direction of the force (the push or pull) that makes it increase or decrease its speed. When you start from rest and pull the accelerometer forward, the cork or bubble moves forward. How can you make the bubble or cork move just a little bit? How can you make it move a lot?

When the accelerometer slows, the force opposes
the motion. The acceleration is negative
(a deceleration). The velocity decreases. The cork or
bubble moves the other way, opposite the motion,
but, as always, it moves in the direction
of the force.

3. Take a walk carrying your accelerometer. Do you
    accelerate and decelerate while walking?

4. Hold the accelerometer at arm's length and turn
    around in a circle several times. What is the direction
    of the acceleration?

5. Take the accelerometer on an automobile or bus ride.
    In what direction is the acceleration when you go
    around a curve? (*Note*: There's nothing wrong with
    the accelerometer. When anything moves in a circle,
    the acceleration is inward toward the center of the
    circle. So is the force.) The inward force that causes
    anything to move in a circle is called a centripetal
    force.

6. Save the accelerometers you have built. You will use
    them in later experiments.

EXPLORING ON YOUR OWN

*   Go on an automobile ride with a parent. Use the speed-
    ometer and a stopwatch to calculate the car's average
    acceleration.

*   Calculate the negative acceleration (deceleration) as the
    car comes to a stop.

- Hold an accelerometer level and note the direction of the acceleration as the car's speed increases and decreases. Note the direction of the acceleration as the car goes around a curve.

THE IMPORTANCE OF GRAPHS IN PHYSICS

Graphs play an integral role in physics. Take a look at Figure 4a. It is a graph that plots distance versus time for a walk like the one discussed in Experiment 1. The slope of this graph (the rise of the line divided by the horizontal run) is 360 ft/60 s or 6 ft/s. As you can see, the slope of the graph is the velocity of the walker.

Figure 4b is a graph of velocity versus time for the walk. It shows that the velocity as a constant 6 feet per second. Since the velocity was constant, the acceleration was zero (except for the initial step).

Acceleration is the slope of a velocity versus time graph. In this case, the slope is zero because the velocity was constant: $\Delta v / \Delta t = 0$. There was no change in velocity.

Notice, too, that the area under this graph, 6 ft/s (the altitude) × 60 s (the length) = 360 ft.

As you can see, the area under a velocity versus time graph is the distance traveled.

Now examine the graph of velocity versus time for a car in Figure 4c. This graph shows a velocity that is increasing at a steady rate for a period of time, then levels off (becomes constant for a time), and then decreases to zero. See if you can answer the following questions.

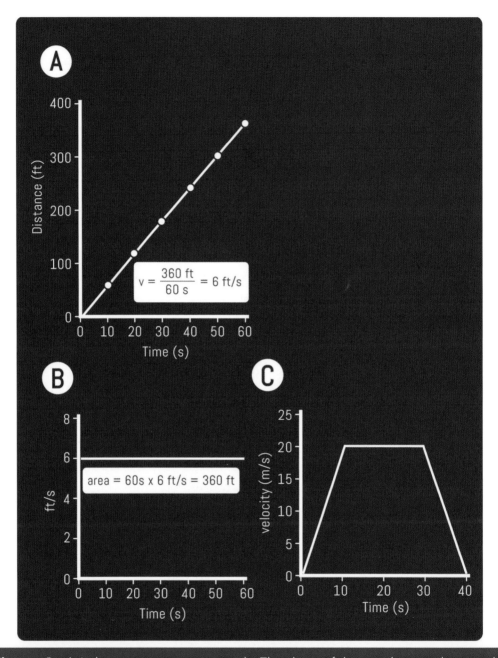

Figure 4. a) A distance versus time graph. The slope of the graph gives the speed. b) A velocity versus time graph obtained from Figure 4a. The graph's slope, $\Delta v/\Delta t$, is zero; hence, the acceleration is zero. The area under the graph is the distance traveled ($d = v \times t$). c) A graph of velocity versus time for a car that traveled for 40 seconds.

1. What is the change in velocity a) during the first 10 seconds? b) during the next 20 seconds? c) during the last 10 seconds?
2. What is the acceleration during a) the first 10 seconds; b) the next 20 seconds; c) the last 10 seconds?
3. How far did the car travel during a) the first 10 seconds? b) the next 20 seconds? c) the final 10 seconds? d) the entire time shown on the graph? (Answers can be found at the end of this chapter.)

The graph in Figure 5 can lead to an equation that can be very useful in finding the distance traveled when there is constant acceleration. Since the acceleration (slope of the graph) is constant, the acceleration, a, is simply v/t. If $a = v/t$, then $v = at$.

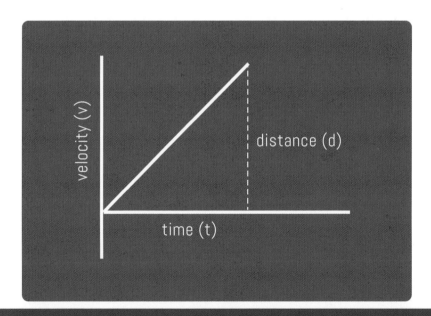

Figure 5. The area under a velocity versus time graph is distance traveled. In this case, the acceleration is a constant so $d = 1/2\ vt$ (area of a triangle). But, since $a = v/t$, $v = at$, and $d = 1/2\ vt = 1/2\ at^2$.

So the distance represented by the area under the graph $(1/2\ vt)$ can be expressed as:

$$d = 1/2\ at \times t = 1/2\ at^2.$$

CONVERSIONS

It would be ideal if the metric system, which is used throughout most of the world, were adopted by the United States. However, physicists work in the real world where units sometimes need to be converted from one system to another.

The conversion of units can be done quite easily using unit analysis. For example, suppose you want to convert 10 miles to kilometers. The value won't change if you multiply by one. And since 1.6 km = 1.0 mi, we can multiply 10 mi by a fraction equal to one and not change its value; consequently,

$$10\ \text{mi} \times \frac{1.6\ \text{km}}{1.0\ \text{mi}} = 16\ \text{km}.$$

Or suppose you want to change 980 centimeters to meters, the same method can be used.

$$980\ \text{cm} \times \frac{1.00\ \text{m}}{100\ \text{cm}} = 9.8\ \text{m}.$$

Some common conversions within and between English and metric systems of measurement are given in Table 2.

Table 2. Some common conversions within and between
English and metric systems of measurement.

Length in English	Length in Metric	Length, English to Metric
5,280 ft = 1 mi = 320 rods	1 km = 1,000 m	1.0 mi = 1.6 km
16.5 ft = 1.0 rod = 5.5 yd	10 mm = 1.0 cm	1.0 in = 2.54 cm = 25.4 mm
36 in = 3.0 ft = 1.0 yd	100 cm = 1.0 m	39.37 in = 3.28 ft = 1.00 m
Area in English	**Area in Metric**	**Area, English to Metric**
43,560 ft2 = 1.0 acre	10,000 m2 =1.0 hectare	1.0 acre = 0.405 hectare 2.471 acres = 1.0 hectare
Volume in English	**Volume in Metric**	**Volume, English to Metric**
16 oz = 1 pt = 0.5 qt	1,000 cm3 = 1,000 mL = 1.0 L	1 qt = 0.946 L = 946 mL 1 gal = 3.785 L
Force in English	**Force in Metric**	**Force, English to Metric**
16 oz = 1.0 lb	1.0 N = 104 dynes	1.0 N = 0.224 lb

SCIENTIFIC NOTATION AND POWERS OF TEN

Writing numbers in scientific notation avoids listing the
many zeros in very small or very large numbers, which are
not rare in physics. Instead of writing 10,000,000, we can
simply write 10^7.

When you multiply numbers using powers of ten, you
simply add the exponents to obtain the answer. Thus, $10^3 \times 10^5 = 10^8$ and $10^3 \times 10^{-5} = 10^{-2}$.

When you divide numbers written in powers of ten, you
subtract exponents. Thus.

$10^4/10^3 = 10^1 = 10$, $10^5/10^8 = 10^{-3}$, $10^2/10^{12} = 10^{-10}$,
$10^5/10^5 = 100 = 1$.

Remember, any number to the zero power is 1.

Any number can be written as the product of a number between 1 and 10 and a power of ten. For example, 35,000 can be written as 3.5×10^4, 0.0025 can be written as 2.5×10^{-3}. Numbers in scientific notation can also be multiplied and divided as shown here. $4.0 \times 10^3 \times 5.2 \times 10^{-6} = 20.8 \times 10^{-3} = 2.1 \times 10^{-2}$.

SIGNIFICANT FIGURES

In the last number, 2.1×10^{-2}, you may wonder why the coefficient was written as 2.1 instead of 20.8. The reason is that the 20.8 was obtained by multiplying 4.0 by 5.2. Those numbers had only two significant figures. Whoever made those measurements, if he or she was paying attention to significant figures, had to estimate the 0 in 4.0 and the 2 in 5.2. The device used to make the measurements, perhaps a ruler, did not allow the person measuring to make any estimates beyond the 0 and the 2. Therefore, any numbers beyond 4.0 and 5.2 would be meaningless and not significant.

Scientific notation allows you to remove any doubt about the number of significant figures and the number of zeros that have meaning. For example, how many significant digits are there in the number 5,700 cm²? If only the 5 and the 7 had meaning, it should be written as 5.7×10^3 cm². If the first zero could be estimated, it should be written 5.70 $\times 10^3$ cm². If all four numbers were significant (only the second zero was estimated), it would be correct to write it as 5.700×10^3 cm^2.

Any calculation using measured numbers should have as many significant figures as the least accurate measurement. For example,

$$\frac{6.34 \text{ g}}{5.7 \text{ mL}} = 1.112 = 1.1 \text{ g/mL}.$$

ANSWERS TO QUESTIONS ON PAGE 25

1. a) 20 m/s; b) 0; c) -20 m/s
2. a) 2 m/s/s or 2 m/s^2; b) 0; c) -2 m/s/s
3. a) 100 m; b) 400 m; c) 100 m; d) 600

CHAPTER TWO

CLASSICAL MECHANICS

Classical mechanics is the study of forces that cause the motion of a mass. (Mass is the amount of matter in body. It is measured in kilograms.) Unlike kinematics, mechanics is interested in what *causes* objects to move.

If you become a physicist, you will also study quantum mechanics, which investigates the forces associated with very small objects such as atoms and subatomic particles.

NEWTON'S LAWS OF MOTION

Sir Isaac Newton (1642–1727) was, perhaps, the greatest scientist of all time. He was the first to really understand motion. During his study of motion, he developed three laws that have come to be known as Newton's first, second, and third laws. They are the basis for much of physics, and every physicist must understand them.

NEWTON'S FIRST LAW

The first law of motion states that a body at rest or in uniform motion (constant velocity) will remain at rest or in uniform motion unless acted upon by an external force (a push or pull). Galileo (1564–1642), another famous scientist, had a similar idea a century before Newton. It was Galileo and others who led Newton to once write, "If I have seen further than other men, it is because I stood on the shoulders of giants."

It was Newton, however, who formulated the laws of motion, which are basic to an understanding of science.

EXPERIMENT 4

NEWTON'S FIRST LAW OF MOTION: BODIES AT REST AND IN MOTION

Most people easily understand the first part of Newton's first law, which states that a body at rest will remain at rest unless acted upon by an external force. Several fun experiments can be done to illustrate this truth.

THINGS YOU WILL NEED

- bottle with a small mouth opening
- table
- scissors
- index card
- marble
- sheet of paper or plastic
- smooth kitchen table or countertop
- plastic cup
- water
- uncarpeted,
- hard surfaced floor
- bouncy ball, such as a tennis ball or Superball
- doll
- toy truck
- incline, such as a board raised at one end
- heavy object, such as a brick
- rubber bands

1. Place a bottle with a small open mouth on a table.
2. Cut an index card in half and place it on the mouth of the bottle.
3. Carefully place a marble on the card directly above the mouth of the bottle (Figure 6a).
4. Snap your finger against one end of the card. The card flies away. What happens to the marble? How does this experiment illustrate Newton's first law?
5. Place a sheet of paper or plastic on a smooth kitchen table or countertop near its edge.
6. Half-fill a plastic cup with water. Place the cup on the paper or plastic near the far end of the sheet as shown in Figure 6b. Hold the part of the sheet that extends from the table with both hands. Pull it very quickly outward and downward. Why does the cup and water remain on the table?
7. Walk along an uncarpeted hard surfaced floor carrying a bouncy ball, such as a tennis ball or Superball. As you walk, drop the ball (Figure 6c). Can you keep walking and still catch the ball? What happens if you stop walking immediately after dropping the ball? How does this experiment illustrate Newton's first law?
8. Place a doll on top of a toy truck. Let the truck roll down an incline, such as a board raised at one end, and crash into a heavy object, such as a brick (Figure 6d). What happens to the doll? How does this experiment illustrate Newton's first law?

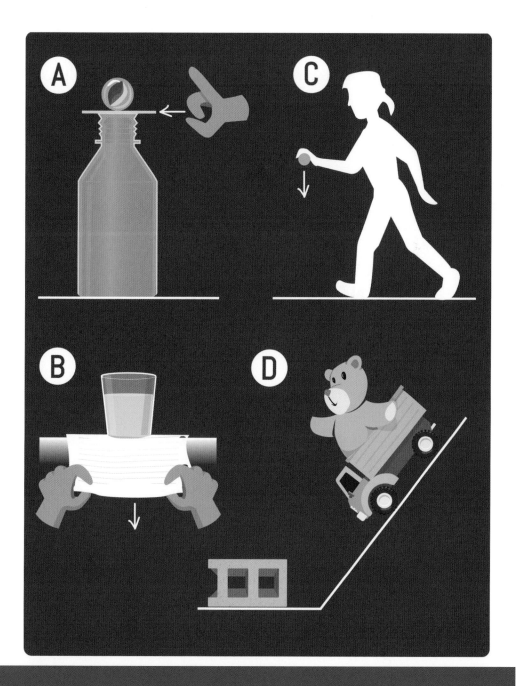

Figure 6. These are some ways to test Newton's first law of motion.

9. Fasten the doll to the truck with rubber bands and repeat the experiment. What happens to the doll this time? Why do you think cars are equipped with seat belts?

EXPERIMENT 5

AN AIR CAR AND WHAT NEWTON IMAGINED

Newton had a vivid imagination. He could visualize motions and experiments that others never considered. He could conceive of motion that illustrated the second part of his first law. Others failed to understand this law because in the real world moving bodies come to rest unless something pushes them. They do not remain in motion.

THINGS YOU WILL NEED

- small nail
- hammer
- metal jar cap
- glue
- empty spool of thread
- balloon
- small wood block
- smooth, level surface such as a counter top

Newton realized moving bodies stop because there is a force—friction—that opposes their motion. In the absence of that force, Newton envisioned that objects moving on a level surface would keep moving. To help you understand motion in his first law, you can build an air car. The car will move with uniform (constant) velocity as long as it is being lifted by air.

1. Using a small nail and a hammer, punch a small hole through the center of the top of a metal jar cap (Figure 7a).
2. Glue an empty spool to the bottom (underside) of the jar cap (Figure 7b). Be sure the holes in the spool and jar cap align.
3. When the glue has dried, pull the neck of an inflated balloon over the top of the spool (Figure 7c). If you have trouble getting an inflated balloon over the neck of the spool without losing most of the air, you can try attaching the balloon in advance and blowing it up from the opposite side using a second spool of thread to blow through. Hold a block against the hole in the jar cap to keep the air from escaping.
4. Remove the block and quickly place the air car on a very smooth, level surface such as a countertop. Give it a little push. Watch it glide along with no further help from you. Does it appear to move at a constant speed? What makes it stop?

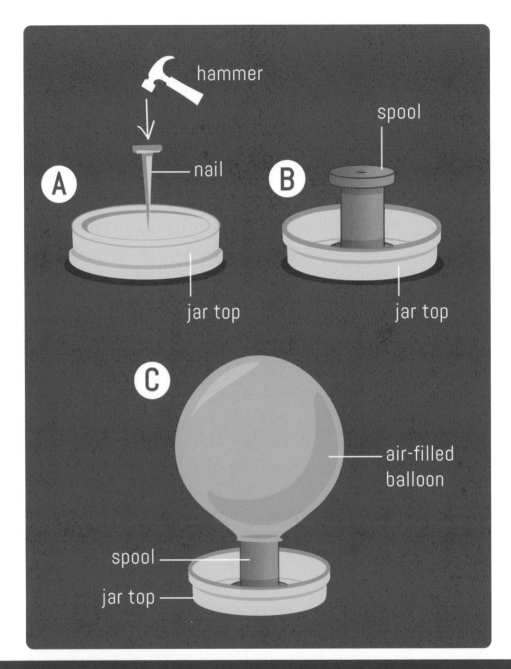

Figure 7. a) Punch a hole in the top side of a metal jar cap. b) Glue an empty spool to the bottom side of the jar top. Be sure the holes align. c) Attach an air-filled balloon to the spool. You have made an "air car." Give it a push so it will move across a smooth, level surface.

5. If you have access to an air hockey table, give one of the pucks a slight push. Watch it move at constant speed across the table.

EXPERIMENT 6

NEWTON'S SECOND LAW

Newton's second law of motion may be stated as follows: When a constant force acts on a mass, the acceleration of the mass is proportional to the force and inversely proportional to the mass. If the units are newtons of force, kilograms of mass, and meters/second/second of acceleration, the law may be stated mathematically: $a = F/m$, or in its more common form, $F = ma$.

The equation $F = ma$ shows us that the units of force (newtons) are equal to kilograms of mass times acceleration in meters per second squared ($\text{kg} \cdot \text{m/s}^2$).

THINGS YOU WILL NEED

- **child's wagon**
- **heavy weights, such as concrete blocks, pails of sand, or other heavy object that can be duplicated**
- **smooth, level surface**
- **spring scale: (0–2000 gram = 0–20 newton)**
- **partner**

In a well-equipped laboratory, it's easy to demonstrate that doubling the force on a mass doubles its acceleration and doubling the mass without changing the force halves the acceleration. Lacking such equipment, you can do a reasonable job of showing the law to be true in a qualitative way.

1. Place a weight in a child's wagon. You might use a concrete block, a pail of sand, or some other heavy object. Be sure you have more than one heavy object that weighs the same.
2. Attach one of the accelerometers you built in Experiment 2 to the wagon.
3. Use a spring scale to pull the wagon along a smooth, level surface at a slow, constant speed. The spring scale allows you to measure the force pulling the wagon. What is the reading on the spring scale when the wagon moves at a steady speed?
4. As you pull, observe the accelerometer. What does the accelerometer indicate?

   Since there is no acceleration, the force is simply overcoming friction between the wagon's wheels and the surface on which they turn. What is the frictional force between the wagon's wheels and the surface?
5. What do you predict will happen if the force you apply to the wagon is *less than* the frictional force? Try it. Was your prediction correct?

6. What do you predict will happen when the force you use to pull the wagon is greater than the frictional force?

7. To check your prediction, use the spring scale to pull the wagon with a force twice as large as the frictional force. Keep the spring stretched to that force as you pull the wagon along the smooth, level surface. What happens to the wagon's velocity as you pull it? What does the accelerometer indicate? Was your prediction correct?

8. What will happen if you apply a force three times as big as the frictional force? Try it! What does the accelerometer indicate?

9. Next, increase the mass in the wagon. Add a second concrete block, pail of sand, or whatever you are using as mass. Measure the force needed to move the wagon along at a steady speed. Does weight affect the friction between the wagon's wheels and the surface?

10. Now pull on this heavier wagon with the same *net force* you applied to the lighter wagon. Remember, the net force is the total force minus the force of friction. For example, if you pulled on the wagon with a force of 200 grams (2.0 newtons) greater than the force of friction when you had one unit of weight in the wagon, do the same now that there are two units of weight in the wagon. That is, pull with a force 2.0 newtons greater than the frictional force on the

wagon. You want the net force to be the same as it was with one unit of weight in the wagon.

Does the added weight of the wagon affect the rate at which the wagon's velocity increases under the same force? If it does, how does it affect it?

You have seen that the wagon accelerates when you apply a force greater than the force of friction. You have seen, too, that the acceleration is greater when the force is greater and smaller when the mass is increased.

NEWTON'S SECOND LAW AND GRAVITY

According to the story, Newton was seated in a yard one day when an apple fell from a tree. At the same time, he noticed the moon above him. He realized that both the apple and the moon were being attracted by Earth's gravity. This observation led him to eventually formulate the law of gravitational attraction. He concluded that there is a force of attraction between any two masses. That force, F (due to gravitational attraction), is proportional to the product of the masses and inversely proportional to the square of the distance, d, between their centers. In mathematical terms:

$F = Gm_1m_2/d^2$. The universal gravitational constant, G, was determined by Henry Cavendish in the 1700s—no small feat for an eighteenth century scientist. Its value is $6.67 \times 10^{-11} \, m^3/kg^2$.

EXPERIMENT 7

GRAVITY AND NEWTON'S SECOND LAW

If masses attract, we would expect Earth, which has a large mass, to attract objects. If it does, it should pull on things and cause them to accelerate. You can do a qualitative experiment to test this idea as well as a quantitative experiment.

If you count to five as fast as you can, it will take you about one second. In this qualitative experiment, you'll use your rapid count as your timer.

1. Hold a ball about one meter or yard above a hard surface.
2. At the moment you release the ball, begin counting as fast as you can. How long did it take for the ball to reach the surface? Repeat several times until you're reasonably confident about the time to fall. It will be less than a second.
3. Repeat the experiment, but this time drop the ball from a height of two meters or yards. If the ball accelerates, it should take less than twice the time it took to fall half as far. If it doesn't accelerate it should take twice as long. What do you find?

4. Now let's do a more quantitative experiment. Figure 8 shows a scaled drawing of a portion of a tape that was attached to a falling mass. As the mass fell, it pulled the tape through a spark timer. The timer produced a spark every 1/60 of a second (0.0167 s). Each spark made a hole in the paper. (Alternating electric current from a power plant has a frequency of 60 cycles per second, which suggests an alternating current was used to make the sparks.)

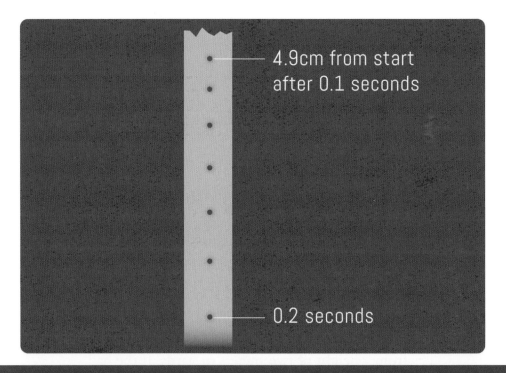

4.9cm from start after 0.1 seconds

0.2 seconds

Figure 8. Part of a copy of a tape that passed through a spark timer that produced a spark every 1/60th of a second. The tape shows the time of fall from 0.1 s to 0.2 s. What was the acceleration of the falling object that pulled the tape through the timer?

After 0.1 second, the object and the tape had fallen 4.9 cm. That distance is the first hole (dot) shown on the tape. The next six holes are shown as the object fell for another tenth of a second (six more sparks). Using the data provided in the tape and a metric ruler, calculate the acceleration of the falling object. Remember $a = \Delta v/\Delta t$.

GRAVITY AND THE VALUE OF G (THE ACCELERATION OF A FALLING BODY ON EARTH)

As Newton showed the world, masses attract with a force, F, given by his law of gravitation: $F = Gm_1m_2/d^2$.

According to this law, what is the force on a mass of 1.0 kilogram near Earth's surface? The answer is found by letting m_1 equal Earth's mass, m_2 equal 1.0 kg, and d equal Earth's radius (6.38×10^6 m).

$F = 6.67 \times 10^{-11}$ m³/kg² $\times 6.0 \times 10^{24}$ kg $\times 1.0$ kg/(6.38×10^6 m)² $= 9.8$ kgm/s².

Since 1.0 kgm/s² is equal to a force of one newton, the answer is 9.8 N.

In Experiment 7 you probably found that the acceleration of the falling body was very nearly 980 cm/s² or 9.8 m/s². So these results agree. Newton's law of gravitation agrees with his second law of motion ($F = ma$). A one kilogram mass, or any mass if we remove air resistance, falls with an acceleration of 9.8 m/s².

Modern timing devices can measure very small time intervals. Experiments using these devices show that over a few meters heavy objects fall with constant acceleration.

Because Earth's gravity varies slightly from place to place, the actual value of the acceleration due to gravity varies slightly with location. At the Panama Canal, close to the equator, the acceleration is 9.782 m/s^2. It is slightly greater at Earth's poles. At the North Pole it is 9.832 m/s^2. In New York and Chicago it is 9.803 m/s^2. The reason for this variation is that the earth is not a perfect sphere. It bulges slightly at the equator. Consequently, Earth's North and South Poles are closer to Earth's center than its equator. Generally, the acceleration due to Earth's gravity is referred to as g. It is generally expressed as 9.8 m/s^2. Using only two significant figures, g is the same everywhere on Earth.

For any mass, its weight is due to the force of gravity, which would cause it to accelerate downward at 9.8 m/s^2. Therefore, the weight of a mass is mg. For most purposes, g is equal to 9.8 m/s^2 or, in engineering units, 32 ft/s^2.

The moon's mass is 7.34×10^{22} kg and the average radius of its orbit as measured from both the moon's center and Earth's center is 3.8×10^8 m. What is the force of attraction between Earth and its moon?

WORK AND ENERGY

Work, W, is defined as a force, F, times the distance, d, through which the force acts, that is:

$$W = F \times d.$$

Energy is defined as the ability to do work, and there are many kinds of energy. Let's look at two.

Suppose you lift a 1.00 kg mass, m, to a height, h, of 1.00 m. The gravitational force on 1.00 kg is 9.80 newtons. (Remember, $F = mg$.) The work you do in lifting the mass is:

$W = mgh = 1.00$ kg $\times$ 9.80 m/s^2 $\times$ 1.00 m $= 9.80$ kg·m^2/s^2 $= 9.80$ Nm or 9.80 joules (9.80J).

The kilogram can do work as it falls. When raised, it has the potential to do work. We say it has potential energy. If allowed to fall, it will accelerate and reach a maximum velocity of 4.42 m/s before colliding with the floor. As it falls, it gains another kind of energy, the energy related to motion, which is kinetic energy (KE). It can be shown that an object's kinetic energy is equal to one-half its mass times its velocity squared; that is to 1/2 mv^2.

Now let's compare the kinetic energy the kilogram mass acquired as it lost the 9.8 joules of potential energy it had gained by being lifted to a height of one meter.

KE $= 1/2$ $mv^2 = 1/2 \times 1.00$ kg $\times$ (4.43 m/s)$^2 = 9.8$ J.

As you can see, the kinetic energy gained equals the potential energy lost. This illustrates the fact that energy is conserved. In any interaction energy is never lost or gained. It may change form but the total energy does not change.

But what about the kilogram mass on the floor? It has lost not only its potential energy but its kinetic energy too. During its collision with the floor, it transferred its kinetic energy to heat (thermal energy). Molecules in the floor and the kilogram mass increased their kinetic energy by a total of 9.8 joules. Numerous experiments have shown this to be true.

As you will learn later in this book, heat, or thermal energy, is the kinetic energy of atoms and molecules.

TERMINAL VELOCITY OF FALLING BODIES

When heavy masses fall short distances, or fall in a vacuum so that air resistance is absent, they accelerate at 9.8 m/s^2.

When falling objects reach high speeds, friction with the air can be as great as the force of gravity. When this occurs, the object no longer accelerates. It reaches a *terminal velocity*—a constant velocity. This is what happens when skydivers jump out of airplanes. They spread their bodies to increase contact with the air and reach a terminal velocity of about 190 kph (120 mph) before opening their parachutes.

NEWTON'S THIRD LAW OF MOTION

Newton's third law states that for every action force there is an equal and opposite reaction force. This might be called the "push, push back law." If I push on you, you push on me whether you want to or not.

EXPERIMENT 8

TESTING NEWTON'S THIRD LAW OF MOTION

Newton's third law applies when you walk. As you walk, your feet push back against the earth. The earth pushes back on you and you move forward. We don't see the earth move because its mass (6 trillion trillion kilograms) is far bigger than yours.

THINGS YOU WILL NEED

- **a partner**
- **skates or skateboards**
- **bicycle helmet**
- **smooth level surface such as ice or a roller skating rink**
- **thin rope about 10 feet long**

The best way to understand Newton's third law is through experience. If you have ice skates, roller skates, or a skateboard—something that greatly reduces friction—you can experience the third law.

1. Stand behind a partner who is also on skates or a skateboard. Make sure you are both wearing bicycle helmets. You should both be motionless on a

smooth level surface such as ice or a roller skating rink. Tell your partner that you are going to give him or her a push.

2. Give your partner a moderate push. Which way does your partner move? Which way do you move? Remember the law, for every action force there is an equal and opposite reaction force.

3. If possible, repeat the experiment with someone much heavier than you. What happens?

4. Again, if possible, repeat the experiment with someone who has less mass than you. What happens? Will the law apply to pulls as well as pushes?

5. To find out, while on skates, use a thin rope about 3 meters (10 feet) long to pull on your partner. Do you move together?

EXPERIMENT 9

OTHER TESTS OF NEWTON'S THIRD LAW

There are many ways to observe the third law of motion. In this experiment you can view some of them.

THINGS YOU WILL NEED

- oblong-shaped balloons
- sink or bathtub
- water
- food coloring
- long string
- soda straw
- twist-tie
- tape
- glass of water
- clay
- string
- spring balance
- sharp pencil
- Styrofoam cup
- scissors
- 2 flexible drinking straws
- thread

1. Blow up an oblong-shaped balloon. Release it. What did the balloon push out through its open end? What pushed back against the balloon?
2. The balloon can push water as well as air. Nearly fill a sink or bathtub with water.
3. Put several drops of food coloring into an oblong-shaped balloon.

4. Attach the balloon to a faucet. Fill the balloon with water. Close the balloon's neck with your fingers and remove it from the faucet.

5. Put the water-filled balloon in the sink or tub and release it. What is the balloon pushing? What is pushing the balloon?

6. Tie one end of a long string to a high point in a room. Run the other end of the string through a soda straw.

7. Fill an oblong-shaped balloon with air and seal its neck with a twist-tie.

8. Tape the straw to the balloon as shown in Figure 9a.

9. Have a partner hold the free end of the string taut as you remove the twist-tie and release the balloon. What happens? How does this experiment illustrate Newton's third law?

10. Place a glass of water on a balance pan. Depending on the type of balance, balance the glass of water with weights, another glass of water, or, if it is an electronic balance, simply record the weight.

11. Attach a large ball of clay to one end of a string. Attach the other end to a spring balance. Predict what will happen to the weight of the clay and to the weight of the glass of water when you lower the clay into the water as shown in Figure 9b.

    Were you right? Did the clay push on the water? Did the water push on the clay? How does this experiment illustrate Newton's third law?

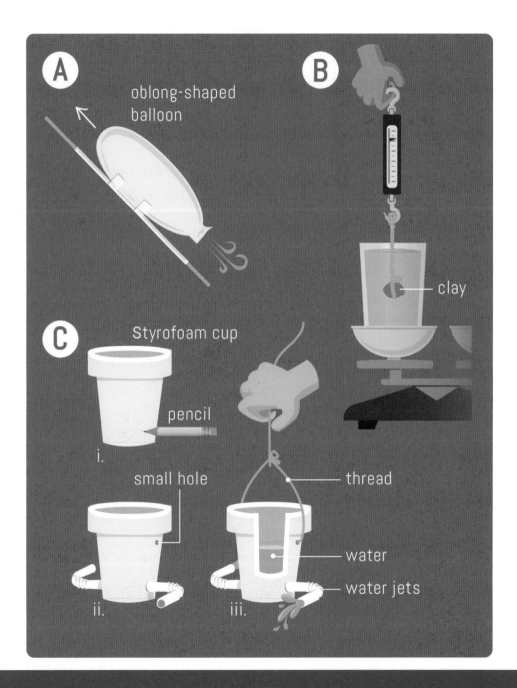

Figure 9. You can test Newton's third law.

12. Make a rotating jet-powered cup fueled by water (Figure 9c). Using a sharp pencil, make two small holes near the bottom on opposite sides of a Styrofoam cup (Figure 9ci).

13. Using scissors, cut the ends off two flexible drinking straws.

14. Push one end of each piece of flexible straw through the holes in the cup. Flex the straws as shown in Figure 9cii.

15. Use the pencil to make two small holes on opposite sides near the top of the cup (Figure 9cii).

16. Run a piece of thread through both holes. Tie the ends to make a loop. Then tie a second piece of thread to the loop so the cup can be suspended (Figure 9ciii).

17. Fill the cup with water in a sink. Hold the end of the support thread as shown in Figure 9ciii.

18. Watch the water "jet" out from the straws. What happens to the cup? How does this experiment illustrate Newton's third law?

19. After the cup has emptied, turn one of the straw jets around so that it points in the opposite direction. Predict what will happen when you repeat the experiment. Were you right?

EXPLORING ON YOUR OWN

- Devise other experiments to test Newton's third law of motion.

- If Earth and the sun attract each other with equal and opposite forces due to gravity, why don't Earth and the sun come together? (Hint: what did you find the direction of acceleration to be when an object moves in a circle?)

MOMENTUM

As you know, when two bodies at rest push on each other, they move apart. During the push (force), each one accelerates and then reaches a final velocity. Each body acquires what is called momentum. Momentum is the product of a body's mass times its velocity, mv. Momentum is produced by a force, F, that acts over a period of time, t. The product force × time (Ft) is known as impulse. So an impulse, Ft, produces a momentum, mv. As you can see, momentum is related to Newton's second law of motion:

$$F = ma = m\ (v/t) \text{ or } Ft = mv.$$

In Experiment 4, when you flicked the card out from under the marble, the marble remained in place because the force on it was very small and very brief. Had you tried to pull the card slowly, the impulse, Ft would have been large enough to give the marble enough momentum to make it move.

The ball you dropped while walking had momentum. Because you were carrying it, it had the same velocity as your body so it retained its forward momentum as it fell and bounced back to your hand.

Like mass and energy, momentum is conserved. When two bodies collide, the total momentum before the collision equals the total momentum after the collision.

CHAPTER THREE

HEAT AND TEMPERATURE

Temperature refers to the hotness or coldness of something. It might be the air, your bath water, or your body. Unlike people who lived a century or more ago, we can regulate the temperature of many objects. Refrigeration allows us to preserve food, and furnaces and air conditioning allow us to control the temperature of buildings. No matter how cold or hot the outside air, we can remain comfortable inside.

In this chapter, you will carry out a number of experiments to help you understand temperature and how it is measured.

EXPERIMENT 10

GALILEO'S THERMOMETER AND ONE LIKE IT

The great Italian scientist, Galileo Galelei (1564–1642), probably made the first thermometer. His thermometer was similar to the one shown in Figure 10a. You can build a workable replica.

THINGS YOU WILL NEED

- **2 clear drinking straws or a length of plastic tubing**
- **scissors**
- **clear tape**
- **soft clay (plasticine)**
- **1-liter or 2-liter clear, empty plastic soda bottle**
- **food coloring**
- **glass or cup**
- **water**
- **a partner**
- **dish towel**
- **hot and cold tap water**

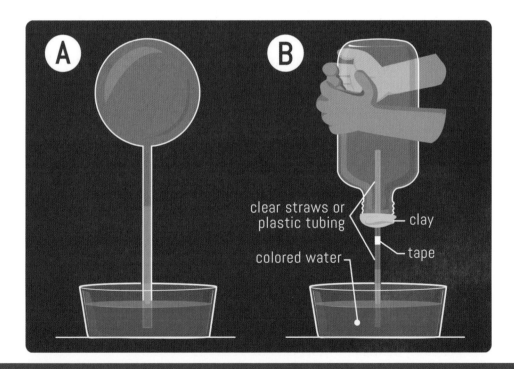

A

B

clear straws or plastic tubing

clay

colored water

tape

Figure 10. a) This air thermometer is similar to Galileo's. b) This is an air thermometer you can build.

1. Put the ends of two clear drinking straws together. Wrap a piece of clear tape around the joint to seal it. (You could substitute clear plastic tubing for the straws.)

2. Push one end of the long straw through a lump of soft clay. The clay should fit around the straw snugly, but it should not squeeze the straw. Make sure the opening of the straw is not clogged with clay.

3. Press the clay into the mouth of a one-liter clear plastic soda bottle. The clay should fill and seal the mouth of the bottle (Figure 10b).

4. Stir several drops of food coloring into a cup of water.

5. Have a partner hold the bottle upside down and put the lower end of the straw or tubing into the colored water as shown.

6. Cover the bottle with a dish towel that has been soaked in hot tap water. Watch the end of the straw or tubing that is in the water. What do you see? How can you tell that the air in the bottle is expanding?

7. After the air stops expanding, remove the towel. Cover the bottle with a dish towel that has been soaked in cold tap water. Watch the colored water move up the straw or tubing. Why do you think water is moving up the tube?

What happens to the water level in your air thermometer when the air temperature decreases? When the temperature increases?

THERMOMETERS AFTER GALILEO

A number of scientists made thermometers that improved on Galileo's design. The biggest difference was that they used a liquid, usually alcohol or a mixture of alcohol and water, instead of air. They sealed the liquid in the tube after removing the air and they added scales to measure temperature.

Using alcohol, or alcohol water mixtures, limited the temperature range that could be measured. These liquids boiled at temperatures well below water's boiling temperature. Also, the volume of some water-alcohol mixtures did not change evenly with changes in temperature.

Reliable and accurate thermometers were made by the German scientist, Gabriel Daniel Fahrenheit (1686–1736), in 1714. Fahrenheit used mercury, a liquid metal, in his thermometers. Mercury remains a liquid well below the freezing temperature of water and well above water's boiling point. Mercury also expands and contracts evenly with changes in temperature.

Fahrenheit made a scale for his thermometer. For zero (0°F), he chose the lowest thermometer reading he could get by putting his thermometer into a mixture of salt, ice, and water. For a high temperature, he chose the temperature of the human body, which he labeled 96°.

Later, he modified his scale. With his thermometer in boiling water, he marked the mercury level as 212°. On this new scale, water froze at 32°; average human body

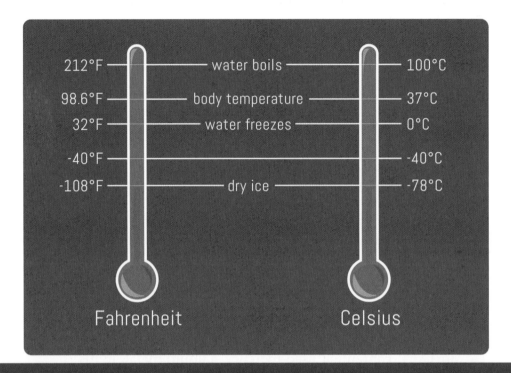

Figure 11. Fahrenheit and Celsius thermometers

temperature was 98.6°. To honor Fahrenheit, we add F to his temperature readings, so average human body temperature is 98.6°F.

The Fahrenheit scale is used in the United States, but most countries and most scientists use a scale invented by a Swedish scientist named Anders Celsius (1701–1744).

Celsius also used mercury in his sealed glass thermometer. On the Celsius scale, water boils at 100°C and freezes at 0°C. Body temperature is 37°C. Figure 11 shows two thermometers, one has the Celsius scale, the other has the Fahrenheit scale.

To convert Fahrenheit temperatures to Celsius, you can use the formula:

$$C = 5/9 \ (F - 32).$$

To convert Celsius temperatures to Fahrenheit, you can use the formula:

$$F = (9/5) \ C + 32.$$

EXPERIMENT 11

A GRAPH FOR CONVERTING TEMPERATURES

A graph of temperature in degrees Fahrenheit versus temperature in degrees Celsius will make it easy to convert one temperature to the other.

THINGS YOU WILL NEED

- **graph paper**

1. Use the formulas above and Figure 11 to prepare a graph of temperature in degrees Fahrenheit versus temperature in degrees Celsius.
2. Save the graph for future use.

EXPERIMENT 12

THE BASIC PRINCIPLE OF A LIQUID THERMOMETER

This experiment will enable you to understand the basic principle behind a liquid-in-glass thermometer. Please reread part 5 of the **Safety First** section of the introduction before doing this experiment.

THINGS YOU WILL NEED

- **an alcohol-in-glass thermometer**

1. Notice the bulb at the base of a liquid-in-glass thermometer. Hold that bulb between your thumb and finger. What happens to the liquid in the thermometer?
2. Hold an ice cube against the thermometer bulb. What happens to the liquid in the thermometer?

    As you have seen, a liquid, like a gas, expands when heated and contracts when cooled.

EXPERIMENT 13

ESTABLISHING FIXED POINTS ON A THERMOMETER

This experiment will help you understand how Celsius and Fahrenheit put fixed marks on their thermometers.

THINGS YOU WILL NEED

- **an adult**
- **safety glasses**
- **oven mitt**
- **plastic cup**
- **crushed ice or snow**
- **water**
- **thermometer (–10 to 110°C or 14 to 230°F)**
- **cooking pan**
- **stove**

1. Half fill a plastic cup with crushed ice or snow. Add a little water and stir gently with the thermometer. Watch the liquid until it stops contracting and remains at a fixed temperature. What is that temperature?

2. Add more crushed ice or snow and continue stirring. Does adding more ice or snow lower the temperature any further? Does the melting point (temperature) of ice or snow (frozen water) depend on mass?

3. Half fill a cooking pan with water. Ask **an adult** to heat the pan of water on a stove with low heat. **Put on safety glasses and hold the thermometer with an oven mitt.**

4. Put the thermometer bulb in the water. **Don't let the thermometer touch the sides or bottom of the pan.** Watch the temperature increase as the water warms.

5. When does the temperature stop rising? What is happening to the water when this happens?

6. Watch the thermometer for several minutes. Does the temperature of the boiling water change? Does mass have any effect on the boiling point of water?

Based on what you have seen in this experiment, why did Celsius choose melting ice and boiling water to determine where to put fixed marks on his thermometer?

TEMPERATURE, HEAT, AND LAWS OF NATURE

Using thermometers, Fahrenheit, Celsius, and others established several laws of nature. Laws of nature are scientific laws based on observations about things and their behaviors for which no exceptions have been found. Such laws allow us to predict what will happen in certain conditions.

Discovering such laws is not enough for true scientists. They want to understand why these laws work. Their explanations for why the laws work are called theories. Good theories not only explain laws, they predict new laws.

JOSEPH BLACK AND A LAW ABOUT TEMPERATURE AND HEAT

A Scottish scientist named Joseph Black (1728–1799) used thermometers to discover some basic laws about temperature and heat. You can do an experiment very similar to one he did more than 250 years ago.

> **THINGS YOU WILL NEED**
>
> - **48-oz (1.4 L) metal can**
> - **cold water**
> - **ice cubes**
> - **spoon to stir ice and water**
> - **at least 2 identical thermometers**
> - **hot tap water**
> - **96-oz (2.7 L) metal can or cooking pan**
> - **watch**
> - **notebook**
> - **pen or pencil**

1. Half fill a 48-oz (1.4 L) metal can with cold water. Add ice cubes until the can is about two-thirds full. Stir ice and water until the temperature is about 0°C (32°F). Then remove any remaining ice.

2. Add hot tap water to a 96-oz (2.7 L) metal can or cooking pan until it is about one-third full.

3. Put a thermometer in each can and record the temperature in each can.

4. Put the cold water can into the can or pan with the hot water.

5. Measure the water temperature in both containers at one-minute intervals. Record those readings in your notebook in a data table like the one below.

Time (minutes)	Temperature	
	Hot Water	Cold Water
start		
1		
2		
3		
. . . .		

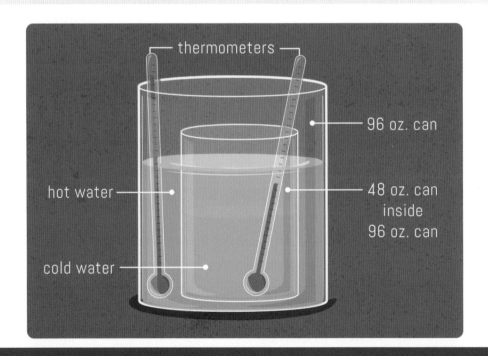

Figure 12. What happens to temperatures when a small can of cold water is placed inside a larger can of hot water?

6. Continue to record temperatures until the temperature in both containers stops changing.

How did the final temperatures in the two containers compare?

When Joseph Black did a similar experiment, he concluded, "We must . . . adopt , as one of the most general laws of heat, that all bodies communicating freely (in contact) with one another . . . acquire the same temperature."

Based on your experimental results, do you agree with Black?

7. Repeat the experiment and again record temperatures every minute. But this time put hot water in the small can and cold water in the big can or pan. What do you predict will happen? Was your prediction correct?

8. Use the temperature data you have recorded to plot graphs of the hot water and the cold water temperatures versus time. Plot time on the horizontal axis and the temperatures on the vertical axis. All the data can be plotted on the same graph. Use one color for the hot water and a different color for the cold water. Connect the data points with smooth curves.

9. Examine the graphs and answer the following questions:

a) When does the temperature change fastest? Slowest?

b) What do the upward and downward slopes of the curves tell you about the rate at which the temperature is changing?

10. Based on experiments similar to yours, Joseph Black proposed three scientific laws:

(1) If objects at different temperatures are in contact, the colder object will get warmer and the warmer object will get colder until their temperatures become equal.

(2) The larger the temperature difference between two objects in contact, the faster their temperatures will change.

(3) The greater the mass of something, the greater the temperature change it can cause in another object and the less will its own temperature change in the process.

Do you agree with the laws proposed by Joseph Black?

BLACK'S THEORY

To explain the laws he had established, Black proposed a theory. According to his theory, heat consists of an invisible, massless fluid that came to be known as caloric. The more caloric within a given volume of matter, the higher its temperature. Adding caloric to matter raises its temperature. The more concentrated the caloric, the higher the temperature. Because of size, a large cold object may contain more caloric than a small hot object.

His theory explains the three laws he discovered. (1) Caloric moves from places where it is concentrated to places where it is less concentrated. It moves until it is spread evenly throughout. (2) The more concentrated the caloric, the faster it flows to an object with less concentrated caloric. (3) The greater the mass of an object, the more heat it can contain. Thus, a large object can hold more heat than a smaller object. It can, therefore, transfer more heat than a less massive object. A large cold object can accept more heat than a less massive one.

EXPERIMENT 15

TEMPERATURE AND HEAT

Joseph Black and other scientists were confused about the difference between heat and temperature (many people are still confused by the same thing). To better understand the difference, they conducted experiments with melting ice that revealed heat and temperature are not the same. You can conduct a similar experiment.

THINGS YOU WILL NEED

- **3 medicine cups**
- **a freezer**
- **measuring cup**
- **hot water**
- **plastic cup (4 to 6 oz)**
- **cold water**
- **one quart (1 L) plastic container**
- **ice cubes**
- **straws**
- **thermometer**
- **two 12 oz foam cups**
- **eyedropper**

1. Fill two medicine cups to the 30-mL (1-oz) line with water. Put both cups in a freezer overnight.
2. Using a medicine cup, get 30 mL (1 oz) of hot water from a faucet. Pour the water into a small (4 to 6 oz) plastic cup.
3. Get 600 mL (20 oz) of cold water from a faucet. Pour it into into a one-quart (1-L) plastic container.
4. Remove the two medicine cups from the freezer. After several minutes, pop the ice out of the cups. Put one into the 30 mL of hot water. Put the other into the 600 mL of cold water. Use separate straws to stir the water in both containers. Which piece of ice melts first? Which water held more heat? Why did it make sense to stir the water?
5. Prepare some ice water. Half fill a one-quart plastic container about half full with cold water. Add ice cubes until the container is about two-thirds full. Stir the ice and water with a thermometer until the water temperature is 0°C (32°F) or nearly so. Remove any remaining ice.
6. Add the ice water to a large (12 oz) foam cup until it is about half full. Be sure there is no ice in the cup.
7. Half fill a second large (12 oz) foam cup with hot tap water.
8. Measure and record the temperature of the hot water and the cold water. Leave the thermometer in the cold water.

9. Using an eyedropper, add one drop of the hot water to the half full cup of cold water. How much did one drop of hot water change the temperature of the cold water?

10. Add ten drops of the hot water to the half full cup of cold water. How much did ten drops of hot water change the temperature of the cold water?

11. Now pour all the remaining hot water into the cold water. How much did the remaining hot water (nearly half a cup) change the temperature of the cold water?

As these two experiments reveal, temperature is not the same as heat. Temperature reveals the degree of hotness or coldness of matter. It does not depend on quantity. Heat, however, involves mass as well as temperature. A large mass of cold water may contain more heat (can melt more ice) than a small mass of hot water.

EXPLORING ON YOUR OWN

- Find ways, not using a cold place such as a refrigerator, to keep an ice cube as long as possible. You might challenge others to an ice-cube-keeping-race. Who can keep an ice cube from melting the longest?
- Make ice with different shapes (cube, cylinder, pancake-shaped cylinder, sphere, cone) from the

same volume of water. Which shape do you think will melt fastest? Slowest? What makes you think so? Try to explain your results.

PROBLEMS WITH THE CALORIC THEORY

Over time it became clear that the caloric theory had many flaws. It was unable to explain why solids are better conductors of heat than gases even though there is more room for the caloric fluid in a gas than in a solid. And it was difficult to accept the idea of a fluid that was weightless and invisible.

The caloric theory was gradually replaced by the kinetic theory. According to the kinetic theory, temperature is a measurement of the average speed of atoms and molecules. Heat is the total kinetic energy of all these particles. The kinetic theory has been successful. It explains temperature and heat without the need of an invisible, weightless fluid.

Although heat is not a fluid, the caloric theory was not completely discarded. A story does not have to be true to teach a valuable lesson. Similarly, a theory does not have to be perfect to be useful. In fact, scientists and engineers routinely use the fluid theory of heat. They talk about heat flowing from place to place as if it were a fluid. Only when the theory no longer makes sense does it become necessary to use the kinetic theory.

EXPERIMENT 16

MEASURING HEAT

In this experiment we define a unit of heat. We'll call our unit a glug and define a glug as the amount of heat produced when an immersion heater operates for thirty seconds after being plugged into an electric outlet. How could you obtain two glugs? Three glugs? Four?

A balance is not needed in this experiment to weigh water. Since a milliliter (mL) of water has a mass of one gram, you can use a graduated cylinder or metric measuring cup to measure grams of water.

THINGS YOU WILL NEED

- **immersion heater**
- **cold water**
- **graduated cylinder or metric measuring cup**
- **foam coffee cups, regular and large (8 and 12 oz)**
- **plastic containers to support foam cups**
- **metric thermometer (°C)**
- **notebook**
- **pen or pencil**
- **electrical outlet**
- **watch or clock that can measure seconds**
- **graph paper**

1. First, check to be sure your heater is consistent. Place 100 grams of cold water in a foam coffee cup that is

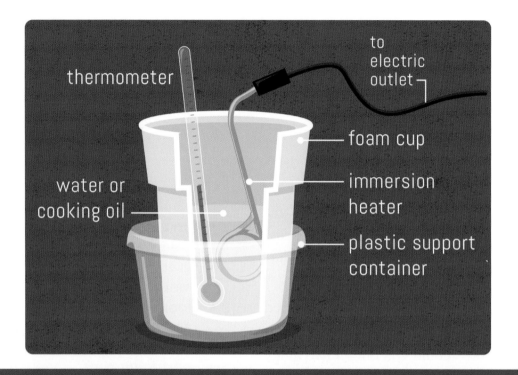

Figure 13. Use an immersion heater to add heat to cold water.

supported by a larger plastic container (Figure 13).

2. Use a thermometer to measure the temperature of the cold water. Record the temperature.

3. Place the heater in the cold water. **Ask an adult** to plug the heater's cord into an electrical outlet for exactly 30 seconds. **(Never plug in the heater unless the coil is in water.)**

4. Do not remove the heater until you have stirred the water with a thermometer and recorded the water's final maximum temperature.

In the figure, the following labels appear: thermometer, water or cooking oil, to electric outlet, foam cup, immersion heater, plastic support container.

5. Repeat the experiment using fresh cold water. Do you obtain very nearly the same results? Is your heater reasonably consistent?

   How do you think the heat delivered to a fixed mass of water will be related to the temperature change of the water?

6. To find out, deliver a glug of heat to 300 g of cold water in a large foam cup.

7. Repeat the experiment using fresh cold water, but this time deliver two glugs of heat to the water.

8. Next, repeat the experiment, but deliver three glugs of heat to the cold water.

9. Repeat the experiment once more and deliver four glugs of heat to the cold water.

10. Record your data in your notebook. Use a table that looks something like this:

Heat (glugs)	mass of water (g)	Initial Temp (°C)	Final Temp (°C)	ΔT (°C)	mass × ΔT (g°C)
1	300				
2	300				
3	300				
4	300				

11. Plot a graph of ΔT versus heat in glugs. What do you conclude?

Suppose the temperature change, ΔT, is kept reasonably constant, how do you predict heat will be related to the mass of water heated?

12. To test your prediction, heat different masses of water with the amounts of heat suggested in the table below. Record all your results in your notebook.

Heat (glugs)	mass of water (g)	Initial Temp (°C)	Final Temp (°C)	ΔT (°C)	mass x ΔT (g°C)
1	300				
2	300				
3	300				
4	300				

Based on your data, is the temperature change reasonably constant? If it is, can you conclude that heat is proportional to the mass of water heated times ΔT?

What do your two experiments suggest is the relationship among heat, mass, and temperature change for water?

Based on the data you have collected, graphs you drew, and relationships inferred, what do you predict will be the relationship between mass of water heated and the water's temperature change if a fixed amount of heat is given to different masses of cold water?

13. To test your prediction, supply a glug of heat to first 100, then 200, then 300, and, finally 400 grams of cold water in a foam cup.

14. Record the temperature change for each run. Plot a graph to test your prediction. Were you right?

15. Using all your data, plot a graph of heat versus the product mass of water × ΔT.

   What do you conclude? Write an equation based on the graph you have drawn.

THE CALORIE: ANOTHER WAY TO MEASURE HEAT

After doing the previous experiment, you probably concluded that heat is proportional to the product of the mass of water heated and its change in temperature. It can be expressed using the equation below.

   Heat = mass of water × change in temperature.

   Scientists came to the same conclusion. They devised a unit of heat that is widely used. That unit is the calorie. A calorie is the amount of heat gained or lost when a gram of water undergoes a temperature change of one degree Celsius.

   1.0 calorie = 1 gram of water × a temperature change of 1.0°C.

   Using data from Experiment 16, how many calories equal one glug?

   Physicists often measure heat in joules. A joule is equal to a newton-meter (Nm). It is a smaller unit than the calorie. 4.18 joules = 1.0 calorie.

EXPERIMENT 17

THE HEAT TO MELT ICE

As Joseph Black discovered, as ice melts, the temperature remains at 0°C even though heat is transferred to the ice. This heat is used to break the bonds that hold the frozen molecules together. Heat that does not cause a change in temperature is called latent or hidden heat.

In this experiment, you can measure the heat needed to melt one gram of ice. It's called the latent heat of fusion.

1. Pour 100 mL (100 g) of water at about 30°C (86°F) into a graduated cylinder.
2. Pour the water into a foam coffee cup. Stir the water and record the water temperature.
3. Wipe an ice cube with a paper towel to remove any melt water on its surface.

4. Add the ice to the water (Figure 14) and stir with a thermometer. It may be necessary to quickly add small pieces of ice you have dried to the water until the water temperature is approximately 10°C. Record the final temperature.

5. Pour the water, which contains the melted ice, into the graduated cylinder. You will probably have to pour twice if you have a 100 mL graduated cylinder. Record the total volume (mass) of the water.

6. Subtract 100 mL from the total volume to find the mass of ice that melted. Record the mass of ice that melted.

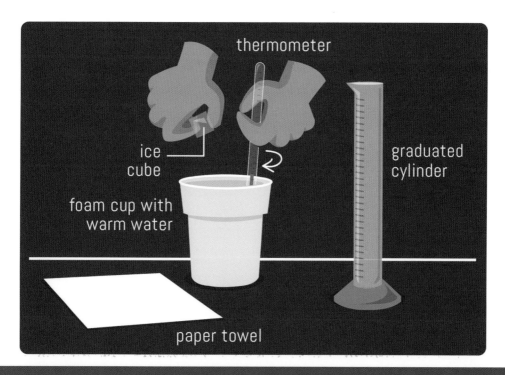

Figure 14. Experiment to find out how much heat, in calories, is needed to melt one gram of ice.

7. To find the heat needed to melt one gram of ice, first calculate the heat lost by the warm water. Suppose the temperature change of the water was 30°C to 10°C, then the heat lost by the warm water was:

$$100 \text{ g} \times 20°C = 2{,}000 \text{ cal.}$$

That heat did two things: (1) It melted the ice, and (2) It warmed the melted ice to the water's final temperature.

Suppose the final volume of water was 122 mL. That would mean 22 g of ice melted (122g – 100g). The heat to warm the melted ice from 0° to 10°C was 22 g × 10°C = 220 cal. The remaining 1,780 calories (2,000 – 220) were used to melt the ice. According to this example, the heat to melt one gram of ice was 1,780 cal/22 g = 81 cal/g.

CHAPTER FOUR

LIGHT AND SOUND

Light and sound are considered together because the behavior of both can be explained by wave transmission. The transmission of sound allows us to hear one another. The transmission of light allows us to see one another. (Of course, we hear and see other things as well.)

Let's begin by examining a model of the waves involved.

EXPERIMENT 18

SOUND WAVES

Sounds are made when something vibrates. The vibrations push on air molecules that push on other air molecules causing the sound to be carried along at a speed in air of about 340 m/s (1120 ft/s) or about 770 mph. Its speed in water is about four times as fast and in a solid like iron its speed is fifteen times as fast as in air. We'll use a model, a Slinky, to show how sound travels.

If you don't have a long Slinky, use twist-ties to fasten several short Slinkies together.

THINGS YOU WILL NEED

- **a long (about 4-5 inches when unstretched), steel Slinky or shorter ones joined together by twist-ties**
- **long, smooth floor**
- **a partner**
- **small piece of yarn**

1. Place the stretched Slinky on a long, smooth floor. Hold on to one end of the Slinky while a partner holds on to the other end.

2. To produce what models a pulse of sound, ask your partner to hold his or her end of the Slinky firmly in place on the floor. Then push your end of the Slinky forward (toward your partner) quickly and then pull it back. Watch the pulse travel along the Slinky to your partner. Does it reflect back toward you after it reaches your partner's fixed hand? Can sound be reflected?

3. As you know, sounds can move from you to a partner at the same time sounds from your partner are moving toward you. It's called "talking at the same time!" Can pulses on a Slinky pass through one another the way sounds do? To find out, have your partner generate a pulse in the same way you do at the same time. Do the pulses pass through one another? Does the

pulse you produced reach your partner? Does your partner's pulse reach you?

4. Your push on the Slinky is a model of the push air molecules receive when a pulse of air is created by a person's vocal chords or by a vibration, like a drum or a bell. To model the multiple sound pulses produced by a vibrating object, repeatedly and rhythmically move the end of the Slinky forward and back while your partner holds the far end in place. Watch the series of pulses move along the Slinky to the other end. When you stop producing pulses, watch the last few you generated. Are they reflected back toward you when they reach the opposite end? Why aren't your words reflected back to you?

A series of evenly spaced pulses creates a longitudinal wave. (See Figure 15a.) Regions where the coils of the Slinky are close together are called compressions. They correspond to increased air pressure where molecules of air are pushed together. The regions where the coils are more widely separated are called rarefactions. They correspond to areas of reduced air pressure where the molecules are less concentrated than normal.

A rarefaction forms when a vibrating object swings back after having pushed molecules together. As it swings back, there is a zone where the molecules are less concentrated because many of the molecules that would normally be there were pushed away to create a compression.

The wave is called longitudinal because it moves lengthwise. It is transmitted by the forward and backward movement of the coils that make up the Slinky. The distance between one compression and the next, or between one rarefaction and the next, is a wavelength. The number of waves generated per second is the frequency of the waves.

Longitudinal waves explain how sound travels from a source to your ear. The vibrating object that produces the sound compresses air molecules. That region of compression then pushes on molecules ahead of it until the wave of compression reaches your ear.

Of course, the Slinky is only a one-dimensional model. In the three-dimensional world sound waves spread out in all directions. We can think of the three-dimensional wave as a huge number of Slinkies carrying sounds outward from a single source of vibration.

5. It is important to realize that although longitudinal waves move along a Slinky or through the air, the coils of the Slinky or the molecules of air simply move back and forth. They carry the wave; they don't move with it. To convince yourself of this, tie a piece of yarn to one coil of the Slinky. Does the yarn move along the Slinky or does it simply oscillate back and forth? Another example of such a wave is the kind that crowds do at sports stadium. The fans all stay in the same place as the wave travels around the stadium.

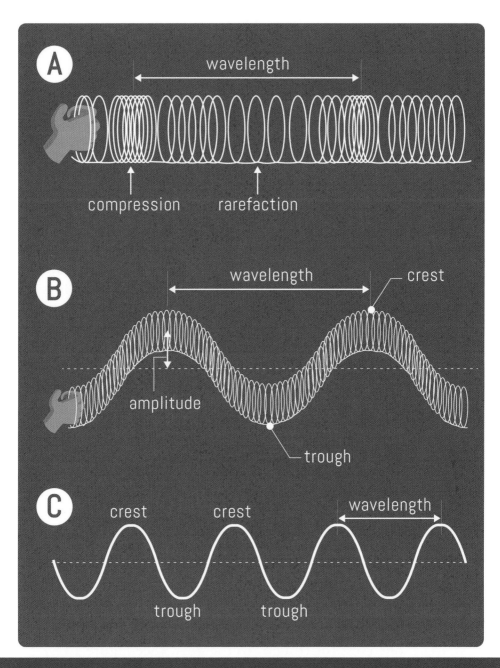

Figure 15. a) A longitudinal wave can be produced on a Slinky. b) The same Slinky can be used to produce transverse waves. c) Transverse waves have crests and troughs. One wavelength is the distance from one crest (or trough) to the next.

EXPERIMENT 19

TRANSVERSE WAVES

Light also travels in waves. But light waves are transverse. They move up and down.

1. To generate a transverse wave move the end of the Slinky quickly to the right and left (side to side) instead of back and forth. Have your partner hold the other end tightly in place. What do these waves look like?

2. The waves you just generated are transverse waves. They move up and down rather than back and forth.

    The amplitude of a transverse wave is the amount the wave moves to either side of its normal position. The wavelength is the distance from one crest (or trough) to the next. (See Figure 15b.)

3. Using the Slinky, make waves with a large and a small amplitude.

4. How can you make waves with a long wavelength? With a small wavelength?

    Are transverse waves reflected when they reach the other end of the slinky? Will transverse pulses or waves pass through one another?

5. Tie a small piece of yarn to the Slinky. Have a partner send transverse pulses down the Slinky. Does the yarn move with the wave or does it simply move back and forth as the wave passes?

    As a transverse water wave passes a floating stick, the stick bobs up and down. It remains in place. It doesn't travel with the wave.

6. Have your partner and you both generate a transverse pulse of about the same size on the same side of the Slinky. What do you predict will happen when the two pulses meet? Try it! Were you right? How can you explain what you saw?

7. With your partner, produce transverse pulses of about the same size on opposite sides of the slinky. Predict what will happen when these transverse pulses meet. You may want to observe this several times. Was your prediction correct?

EXPERIMENT 20

SOUND WAVES AND A HORN

When you launch a longitudinal wave on a Slinky, the coils move back and forth about a central position. They do not move along the Slinky with the wave. We used the Slinky as a model for sound and light waves. That model suggests that while sound waves travel outward from a source, the air itself simply oscillates like the coils of a Slinky.

THINGS YOU WILL NEED

- **bugle or a similar wind instrument**
- **a partner**
- **bubble-making solution**
- **a shallow wide dish**
- **large room**

1. Let's use a bugle or a similar wind instrument to see if the air that transmits sound moves with the sound waves or simply oscillates like the Slinky. If you can play a bugle or another wind instrument, you can find out. If you don't play such an instrument, ask a partner who does to help you.

2. Pour bubble-making solution into a shallow, wide
    dish. Then dip the wide end of the horn into the
    solution.

    Blow a few notes on the instrument. Watch the
    bubble at the end of the horn. Can you or a part-
    ner hear sound on the opposite side of the room?
    Does the air in the bubble at the end of the horn
    move to the opposite side of the room, or does it
    remain in the bubble?

SOUND WAVES AND LIGHT WAVES

The best human ears can hear sounds with a frequency as
low as 20 Hertz and as high as 20,000 Hertz. Hertz (Hz)
is a measure of frequency, one Hertz equals one wave per
second.

The velocity of sound, and of light, can be measured if
we know two of the following three variables: wavelength,
velocity, and frequency.

Wavelength is usually represented by the Greek letter
lambda, λ, frequency by the letter f. It follows that the velocity, v, of waves is given by $v = \lambda f$ and so $\lambda = v/f$ and $f = v/\lambda$.

If something has a wavelength of 10 m and a frequency
of 10 per second the velocity must be 100 m/s because 10
waves, each with a length of 10 m, pass by a fixed point in
one second.

A beam of red light might have a wavelength of $6.5 \times
10^{-7}$ m. We know that light travels at a speed of 3.0×10^{8}

m/s so the frequency of the light is:

$$f = v/\lambda = 3.0 \times 10^8 \text{ m/s} / 6.5 \times 10^{-7} \text{m} = 4.6 \times 10^{16}$$

per second.

You can see why physicists found it easier to measure the speed of light and its wavelength rather than its frequency.

About a century ago, Albert Michelson measured the speed of light with great precision by reflecting a beam of light over a large distance. It was very close to 3.0×10^8 m/s.

Sound waves travel through air at a speed of about 340 m/s at 20°C. The wavelength of the lowest frequency (20 Hz) that a human can hear is:

$$\lambda = v/f = 340 \text{ m/s} / 20 = 17 \text{ m}$$

The wavelength of the highest frequency (20,000 Hz) that a human can hear is:

$$\lambda = v/f = 340 \text{ m/s} / 2.0 \times 10^4 = 1.7 \times 10^{-2} \text{ m} = 17 \text{ mm}.$$

EXPERIMENT 21

THE LAW OF REFLECTION

When light strikes a mirror or any other reflective surface, it is reflected. In this experiment we'll examine the angle at which light strikes a mirror and the angle at which it is reflected.

THINGS YOU WILL NEED

- heavy black construc- tion paper
- ruler
- shears
- a room that is dark
- clear 60-watt bulb with a small visible filament or a clear lightbulb such as a tubular
- showcase bulb with one long vertical filament
- clay
- mirror
- sheet of white paper
- protractor
- long table or two small tables

1. To make a single slit ray maker, use a sheet of heavy black construction paper. Using shears, cut a piece from the paper that is about 10 cm (4 in) × 15 cm (6 in).

2. Find the center of one long side. At that point use scissors to carefully cut a narrow (1 mm wide) verti- cal slit. Make the slit about 6 cm (2.5 in) long. (See Figure 16a.)

3. Fold about 3 cm (1.5 in) of the paper at each end so it will stand upright (Figure 16a).

4. In a room that is quite dark, set up the experiment as shown in Figure 16. Use either of the clear light- bulbs mentioned above. Place the lightbulb about one meter (100 cm) or a yard from the black upright paper.

5. Stick a piece of clay to the back of the mirror to keep it upright on a sheet of white paper.

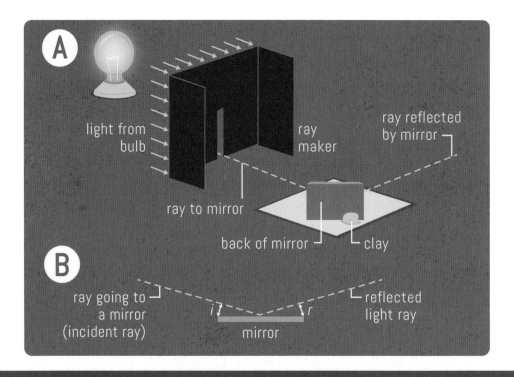

Figure 16. a) A ray maker can be used to produce narrow beams (rays) of light. b) How does angle A compare with angle B when a light ray is reflected by a mirror?

6. Turn on the light. The narrow beam (ray) of light coming through the slit should reflect from the mirror.

7. To change the angle at which the light ray hits the mirror, turn the mirror.

   The ray coming from the light to the mirror is called the incident ray. The light that is reflected is the reflected ray.

8. Use a protractor to measure the angle between the incident ray and the mirror (angle *i*). Use the same

protractor to measure the angle between the reflected ray and the mirror (angle r). Be sure the center of the protractor's base is at the point where reflection takes place.

How do the two angles (i and r) compare?

9. Turn the mirror to change the angle between the incident ray and the mirror. Measure angle r for many different values of angle i. How do the two angles compare?

You have found a scientific law—something that is always true. How would you state your law? What would you call it?

You probably found that angles i and r were always equal (or nearly equal) for all values of angle i. That is the law of reflection. When light is reflected, the angle of incidence equals the angle of reflection.

EXPERIMENT 22

WHERE IS YOUR MIRROR IMAGE?

Look into a mirror. Where does your image appear to be? Is it on the mirror's surface? Where do you think it is? Do an experiment to find out.

1. Here is a way to locate a mirror image. Suppose two things are at the same place. They will stick together when you move your head from side to side, or when you close one eye and then the other.

If they are not at the same place, the closer one will appear to move more relative to the one farther away. Astronomers would say there is parallax. Parallax is the apparent displacement of an object due to a change in the position of the viewer (right eye versus left eye). In astronomy, a star may appear to shift position when viewed from different positions along Earth's orbit.

2. To experience parallax, hold one finger in front of you at arm's length. Hold another finger close to your face. Look at both fingers. Look first with your right eye, then with your left eye. You'll see the nearer finger shift a lot relative to the distant finger.

3. Now hold one finger on top of the other at an arm's length. Again, close first one eye and then the other. This time the fingers stay together. They

do not shift relative to one another because they are at the same place.

4. Place a short pencil about 10 cm (4 in) in front of a small mirror (Figure 17a). The pencil should be about as tall as the mirror. Use small lumps of clay to support the pencil and the mirror.

5. Hold a taller pencil behind the mirror.

6. Put your head behind the pencil in front of the mirror. Look at the pencil in front of the mirror. You can see its image in the mirror. And you can see the top of the second pencil behind the mirror.

7. Move the pencil behind the mirror to different positions. Keep it in line with the *image* of the pencil in front of the mirror. At each position, look first with your right eye and then with your left eye. Keep moving the pencil slowly and closing your eyes. Do this until the image and the tall pencil show no parallax (stick together). Now you know the tall pencil is at the same place as the *image* of the short pencil.

8. Measure the distance from the mirror to the pencil in front of the mirror. Then measure the distance from the mirror to the pencil behind the mirror (the position of the image). How do these distances compare? When you look in a mirror, where is your image?

Although mirror images are behind the mirror, many people do not believe it. You, however,

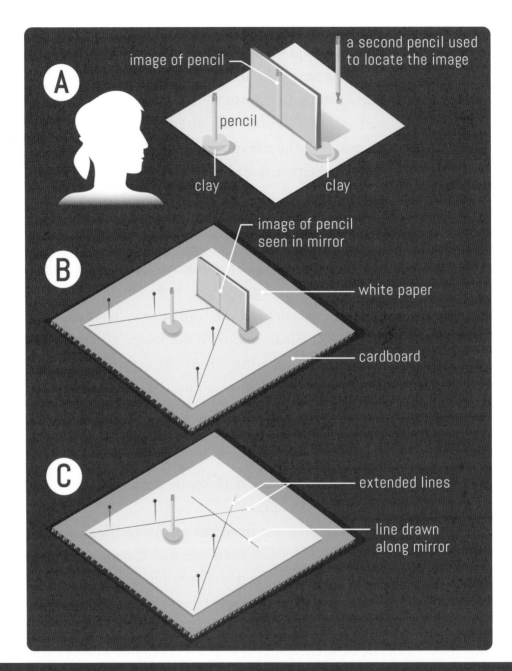

Figure 17. a) Use parallax to locate the image seen in a plane mirror. b) Use pins to form sight lines (rays) to the mirror image. c) Remove the mirror. Extend the sight lines until they meet at the location of the image you saw.

proved the images really are there. Of course, you can't find an image behind the mirror. The reason is that the image is a virtual image. A virtual image is one that seems to be in a certain place because of the way light rays from the object creating the image are reflected. Figures 17b and 17c show how a virtual image is formed by reflected rays.

9. To see this for yourself, use 4 pins to form two sight lines (rays) to the image as shown in Figure 17b. Then draw a line along the front of the mirror to mark its position.

10. Remove the mirror. Using a ruler, draw lines defined by the pins marking the reflected rays. Extend the lines until they meet. Where do they meet?

EXPLORING ON YOUR OWN

- How tall does a mirror have to be to create a full length image of you?
- Examine the images formed by a concave mirror, such as a makeup mirror. Where are the images? How does it depend on the position of the object that makes the image?
- Examine the images formed by a convex mirror. Where are they? Does it depend on the position of the object that makes the image?

EXPERIMENT 23

REFRACTION OF LIGHT

When you look into a swimming pool, the water doesn't look as deep as it really is. The reason is that light refracts (bends) when it passes from one clear substance to another. The light emerging from the water bends as it enters the air. To see exactly how light refracts (bends), you can look at a ray of light as it enters water from air.

Light bends (refracts) when it enters water at an angle. You can compare the angle of incidence of a light ray approaching a liquid with the angle of refraction of the same ray after entering the liquid. (See Figure 18a.)

THINGS YOU WILL NEED

- **white paper**
- **cardboard sheet**
- **clear, rectangular, plastic container about 10 cm (4 in) × 5 cm (2 in) × 5 cm deep**
- **water**
- **sharp pencil**
- **large pins such as T-pins**
- **ruler**
- **protractor**
- **nondairy creamer**
- **laser pointer**

1. Lay a sheet of white paper on a cardboard sheet. Place a clear, rectangular, plastic container near the center of

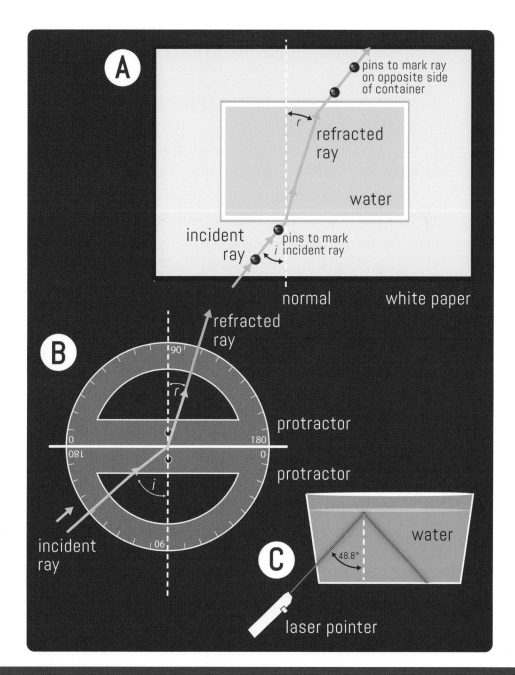

Figure 18. Use a ruler and pencil to draw the incident and refracted light rays. b) Use a protractor to measure the angle of incidence (i) and refraction (r). c) Find the approximate critical angle for light passing from water into air.

the paper. Nearly fill the container with water. Mark the sides of the container on the paper with a sharp pencil.

2. Use two pins to define an incident ray to the water as shown in Figure 18a.

3. Go to the other side of the container. Line up two more pins with the first two you placed on the opposite side of the container.

4. Carefully remove the container of water. Use a ruler to draw the two light rays defined by the pins. You can probably see that the two rays are parallel but not in line with one another. Light entering the water is bent (refracted) toward the normal (a line perpendicular to the water at the point the light enters the water). It is refracted away from the normal when it leaves the water and enters air.

   Light travels in straight lines. Therefore, the path that the light must have followed in the water is the line connecting the points where it entered and left the water.

5. Draw that ray on the paper. Use a protractor to measure the angles of incidence and refraction as shown in Figure 18b. How do they compare? What is the ratio of angle i to angle r?

6. Repeat the experiment for a number of different angles of incidence. Try to go from angles of about 20 degrees to 80 degrees. You may find it hard to see the incident pins through the water at large angles of incidence. Do the best you can. Is the ratio of angle i

to angle *r* constant, or does it change as the angle of incidence grows larger?

As you have seen, light bends toward the normal when it enters water and away from the normal when it passes from water into air. Suppose you were to gradually increase the angle of a light beam going from water into air. Eventually, the beam would leave the water at an angle of 90 degrees. What would happen if you increased the angle a little more?

7. To find out, add a pinch of nondairy creamer to a clear, deep, water-filled, plastic container.

8. Stir to spread the creamer throughout the water. Then, **under adult supervision**, shine a pencil laser into the cloudy water as shown in Figure 18c. What happens when the angle of the beam in the water approaches 49 degrees?

At 48.8 degrees, all the light is reflected. None of the light leaves the water and enters the air. This is known as total internal reflection and 48.8 degrees is called the critical angle for light passing from water into air.

EXPLORING ON YOUR OWN

- Design and carry out an experiment to measure the angles of incidence and refraction when light passes from air to glass. Does glass bend light more, less, or the same as water? Does clear plastic bend light more, less, or the same as water?

EXPERIMENT 24

REFRACTION OF LIGHT BY A CONVEX LENS

Lenses refract (bend) light. If you feel the surface of a convex lens, you will discover it is curved. It bulges outward in the middle. Concave lenses are thinner in the middle and thicker at their perimeters. (See Figure 19a.)

1. As Figure 19b shows, a convex lens converges light (brings it together). The point where parallel light rays come together is the focal point of the lens. The distance from the

THINGS YOU WILL NEED

- **an adult**
- **convex lens with a focal length of 15–30 cm (a magnifying glass)**
- **clay**
- **meterstick or yardstick**
- **file card**
- **matches**
- **candle**
- **table**
- **a partner**
- **sheet of white cardboard**
- **concave lens**
- **black paper single slit ray maker used in Experiment 21**
- **clear 60-watt bulb with a small visible filament or**
- **a clear lightbulb such as a tubular showcase bulb with one long vertical filament**

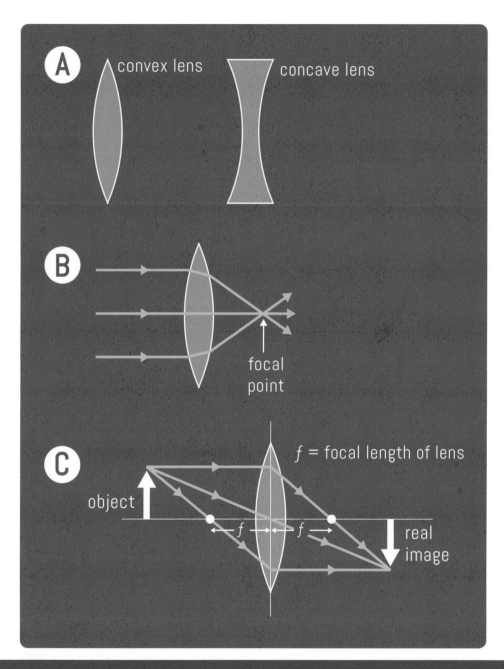

Figure 19. a) Convex and concave lenses. b) A convex lens can bring parallel light rays together to at the lens's focal point. c) A convex lens can form real images of objects that are more than one focal length from the lens.

center of the lens to the focal point is the focal length of the lens.

2. This convergence of light suggests that a convex lens can bring together light from an object to form an upside-down (inverted) image of the object (Figure 19c).

3. To see if this really happens, find a light colored wall opposite a window with a view of the outside. Hold a convex lens near the wall. Can you form images of the view on the wall? Are the images inverted?

   The images you see are real images. Unlike the virtual images you see in a plane mirror, these images are really there. They can be seen on a screen.

   The focal point of a convex lens is the point where parallel rays of light are brought together. To obtain parallel rays of light, you can use a distant object such as a tree, a mountain, a tall building, or any object that is distant. Light rays from a distant object must be very nearly parallel. Any diverging rays would not strike the lens.

4. To find the focal length of your convex lens, fix the clear image of a distant scene on a wall. Measure the distance between the center of the lens and the image. What is the focal length of your convex lens?

5. To see if the focal length on both sides of a convex lens is the same, simply turn the lens around. Has the focal length changed?

6. In a dark room, **with an adult present**, light a candle on a table. Place a convex lens more than one focal length from the candle.

7. Have a partner use a sheet of white cardboard to locate the image of the candle flame. What do you notice about the image?

8. Place the lens exactly two focal lengths from the candle. What is the distance between the lens and the image?

9. What happens to the size and location of the image as you move the lens closer to the candle? As you move the lens farther from the candle?

10. What happens when you place the lens less than one focal length from the candle?

11. Look toward the candle through the lens. The image you see when you hold the convex lens less than one focal length from the candle is a virtual image. It is similar to the images you see in a plane mirror. It appears to be where it is because your eye assumes the diverging rays originate where they appear to join at a point on the other side of the lens as shown in Figure 20.

12. Hold the convex lens a few centimeters above the print on this page. How does the size of the virtual images you see compare with the size of the print? Can you explain why?

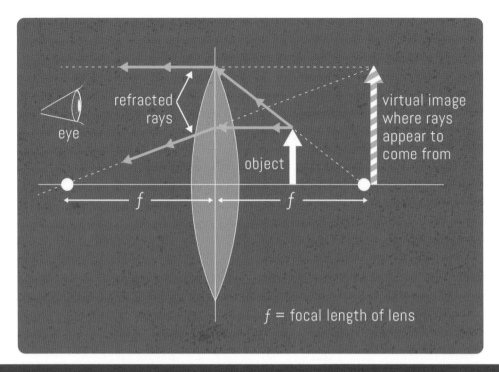

refracted rays

eye

object

virtual image where rays appear to come from

f

f

f = focal length of lens

Figure 20. When an object is less than one focal length from a convex lens, its image will be virtual. It will be located at a point where the refracted rays appear to originate.

13. If possible, look at objects through a concave lens. All images you see are virtual because a concave lens diverges (spreads) light. Light rays passing through such a lens will never come together.

MODELING A CONVEX LENS

14. Using scissors, make a second narrow slit in the single-slit black-paper ray maker you made before. Make the two slits about a centimeter apart. A jar of water can serve as a model of a convex lens. See Figure 21.

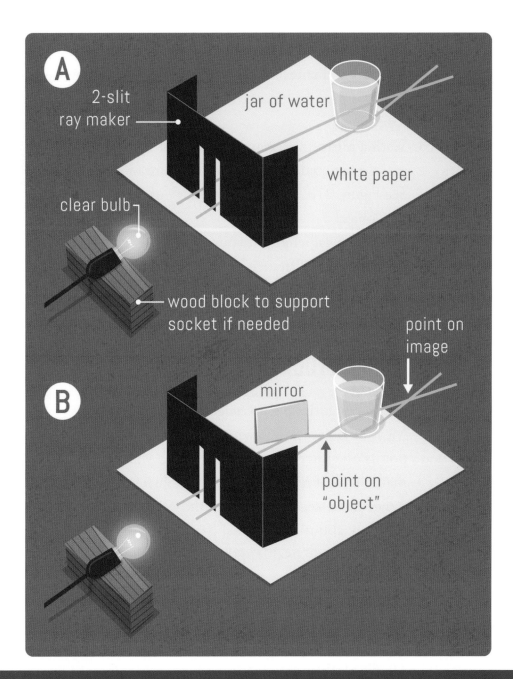

A
2-slit ray maker
jar of water
white paper
clear bulb
wood block to support socket if needed

B
mirror
point on image
point on "object"

Figure 21. a) A model of a convex lens. b) A better model showing how one point on an object becomes one point on an image. A mirror reflects one ray to form a point on an "object."

15. Let light from the clear lightbulb pass through the two slits and enter the water-filled jar. Notice that the light rays are refracted by the "lens" and brought together.

16. With a mirror, you can reflect one of the rays to make what could be light from a point on an object. See Figure 21b. Where is the image of the point on the "object"?

17. Find the focal length of your cylindrical lens. What happens as the distance between object and lens changes? What happens when the object is less than a focal length from the lens?

EXPLORING ON YOUR OWN

- Make a quantitative investigation of a convex lens. Measure object and image distances from the focal points on either side of the lens. Can you find a mathematical relationship among object distance, image distance, and focal length?

  How about a relationship among object height, image height, focal length, image distance, and object distance?

- Design a method for locating the position of the virtual images seen through a concave lens.

CHAPTER FIVE

ELECTRICITY AND MAGNETISM

During the first forty years of the twentieth century, the United States became electrified. Earlier, most street lights were fueled by gas and home lighting was supplied by candles or oil lamps. In this chapter, you will do some basic experiments pertaining to electricity and magnetism. We'll begin with a simple but revealing experiment.

Warning: Do not experiment with the electricity in your home!

EXPERIMENT 25

A BATTERY, BULB, AND WIRE

Given a D-cell (battery), flashlight bulb, and a copper wire, in how many ways can you light the bulb?

THINGS YOU WILL NEED

- **D-cell**
- **flashlight bulb**
- **a copper wire**

1. Using the D-cell, bulb, and wire, in how many ways can you make the bulb light?

EXPERIMENT 26

A SERIES CIRCUIT AND A PARALLEL CIRCUIT

Electrical elements, such as lightbulbs, radios, and TVs can be connected in series (one after the other) or in parallel (side by side). Do you think it will make any difference? Let's find out.

1. If you have battery and bulb holders and alligator clips, you can use them to build circuits (Figure 22a). If not, you can make your own equipment as shown in Figure 22b.

2. Symbols can be used to show circuit

THINGS YOU WILL NEED

- **battery holders**
- **bulb holders**
- **alligator clips**
- **insulated wires or paper clips**
- **rubber bands**
- **thumbtacks**
- **wood blocks**
- **clothespins**
- **D-cells**
- **flashlight bulbs (use bulbs that light when connected to one D-cell)**

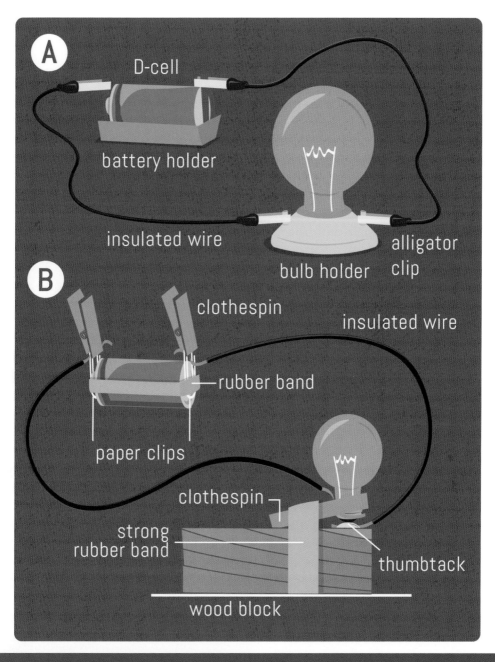

Figure 22. a) An electric circuit is easy to build if you have battery and bulb holders and wires with alligator clips. b) You can make your own battery and bulb holders using paper clips, rubber bands, thumbtacks, wood blocks, and clothespins.

elements and their connections. Those symbols are shown in Figure 23a through 23k.

3. Build the series circuit shown in Figure 23i. Note the brightness of the bulbs.

4. Now build the circuit shown in Figure 23j. It consists of a single bulb. How does the brightness of this bulb compare with the brightness of the two bulbs in series?

5. Build the parallel circuit shown in Figure 23k. How does the brightness of the bulbs compare with the single bulb circuit? With the bulbs wired in series?

MORE ABOUT CIRCUITS

Ammeters are used to measure electric current. An electric current is the flow of charge (usually electrons) along a circuit.

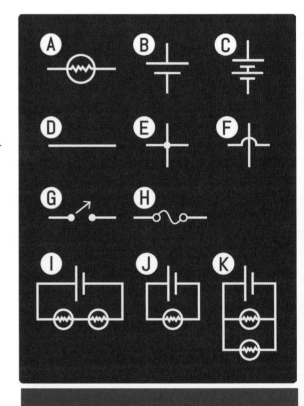

Figure 23. In drawing electric circuits, the parts may be represented by these symbols. a) a bulb; b) an electric cell (battery); c) two cells connected head (+) to tail (–); d) a wire; e) wires that are joined; f) wires that cross but are not joined; g) a switch; h) a fuse; i) series circuit; j) simple circuit; k) parallel circuit.

If you have an ammeter and a voltmeter, you can rebuild the circuits as shown in Figure 24. Notice that the ammeter is in series with any circuit element; the voltmeter is in parallel with circuit elements for which the voltage is to be measured.

An ammeter measures current in amperes. One ampere is a flow of charge equal to one coulomb of charge per second. A coulomb consists of 6.24×10^{24} electric charges (usually electrons).

A voltmeter measures the energy per charge in volts. And one volt is one joule (newton-meter) per coulomb.

Ammeters offer very little resistance to the flow of charge. Therefore, they can be wired in series with circuit elements. The current through the ammeter will be almost exactly the same as the current through the circuit element in series with the ammeter

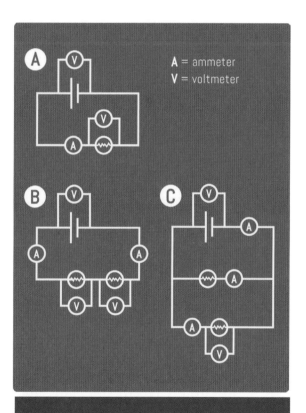

Figure 24. If you have a DC (direct current) ammeter and a DC voltmeter you can measure currents and voltages for the circuits shown. Meters can be moved to different places in a circuit. Only one ammeter and one voltmeter are needed.

Very little current flows through a voltmeter because it offers a large resistance to the flow of charge. Consequently, adding a voltmeter in parallel with a circuit element has negligible effect on the current elsewhere.

EXPERIMENT 27

MAGNETS AND A MAGNETIC COMPASS

You have probably played with magnets, so you know that like poles (north and north or south and south) will repel one another, but unlike poles (north and south) will attract.

A compass needle is a small magnet. One end will point in a northerly direction. You may have heard that it points toward the North Pole. Not true! It points to the North, but not usually toward the North Pole. It points toward Earth's magnetic South Pole, which is located near the Boothia peninsula in northern Canada, about 1,200 miles (1,931 km) from the North Pole.

Earth's magnetic North Pole is in Antarctica. Remember, opposite poles attract.

1. Examine a magnetic compass. Are the ends of the compass needle (a small magnet) labeled N and S? Does the north end of the needle point in a northerly direction? (Be careful, sometimes the poles become reversed if a strong magnet is brought too close to the compass.)

2. Slowly bring a bar magnet near the compass. Is the north pole of the needle attracted to the magnet's south pole? Is it repelled by the magnet's north pole?

3. To make a large magnetic compass, hang a bar magnet from a ceiling or some high point. When the magnet comes to rest, in which direction does the magnet's north pole point?

EXPERIMENT 28

OERSTED'S DISCOVERY AND AMPERE'S RULE

For many years, scientists felt there must be a connection between electricity and magnetism. There were positive and negative electric charges. Like charges repelled, and unlike charges attracted. Magnets had north- and south-seeking poles. Like poles repelled, and unlike poles attracted. Despite these similarities, magnets and electric charges seemed to have no effect on one another. But then, in 1819, Danish physicist Hans Christian Oersted (1777–1851) discovered a connection. You can make the same discovery that Oersted made about 200 years ago.

1. Put a magnetic compass on a non-metallic surface such as a wooden table.
2. Lay a long, straight, insulated wire with connecting clips at each end on top of the compass. Be sure the wire is parallel to the compass needle (Figure 25a).
3. Connect one end of the wire to one electrode of a D-cell. Briefly touch the other end of the wire to the other electrode. What happens to the compass needle?
4. Place the wire under the compass and repeat the experiment. What happens? What is the same? What is different?
5. Reverse the wire's connections to the battery. What happens? What does this tell you about the connection between an electric current and magnetism?

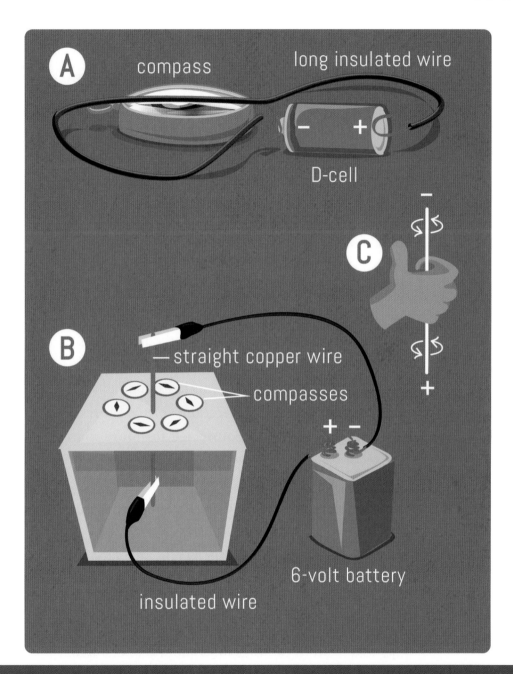

Figure 25. a) What did Oersted discover about the link between electricity and magnetism? b) What does the magnetic field around an electric current look like? c) The right-hand rule gives the direction of the magnetic field around a current.

A week after Oersted's discovery was published, André Ampère (1775–1836), a French physicist, devised a rule. This rule enabled anyone to predict the direction of the magnetic field around an electric current. An experiment will show you how Ampère arrived at his rule.

6. Push a long, straight piece of heavy copper wire through one end of a cardboard box. See Figure 25b. If you have several magnetic compasses, place them around the wire as shown. (You could use iron filings rather than compasses.) If you only have one compass, ask a partner to slowly move the compass around the wire. Watch the compass as you do the next step.

7. Using insulated wires with clips, briefly connect the ends of the long wire to a 6-volt lantern or alkaline battery as shown. The connections form a short circuit so **it should not be connected for more than a few seconds**. The compass needles point in the direction of the magnetic field.

   As you can see, the magnetic field forms a circular pattern around the electric current.

8. The direction of the field lines can be predicted by Ampère's "right hand rule." Point your right thumb in the direction positive charge would flow in the wire (+ to –). Your fingers curl in the direction of the magnetic field (S to N) around the wire. See Figure 25c. It shows the direction north-seeking poles would point. Do your results agree with this rule?

DIRECTION OF ELECTRIC CURRENT

The direction of electric current is defined as the direction that positive charge would flow—from a positive electrode to a negative electrode. This definition came from Benjamin Franklin. He thought of electricity as a fluid. It seemed reasonable that lots of fluid, which he called positive, would flow to less fluid, which he called negative. Today, we know that it is the negative charges (electrons) that actually move through wires.

How would you modify Ampère's rule if electric current were defined as the direction that negative charge flows—from a negative electrode to a positive electrode?

EXPERIMENT **29**

PRODUCING AN ELECTRIC CURRENT USING A MAGNET

If an electric current can produce a magnetic field, it seemed reasonable that a magnetic field should be able to produce electricity. It was the great English scientist, Michael Faraday (1791–1867), who first demonstrated that this can be done. In this experiment, you will do something similar to Faraday's experiment.

THINGS YOU WILL NEED

- long insulated connecting wires with alligator clips
- galvanometer or microammeter to show electric current
- coil (about 5 cm in diameter) made of enameled copper wire that has at least 50 turns
- clay to support the coil
- strong magnet
- a partner

1. Use sandpaper to remove the enameled insulation from the two ends of the wire coil. Then use long insulated wires to connect the two ends of the coil to the + and − leads of a galvanometer or microammeter. See Figure 26.

2. Hold the strong magnet near the coil of wire. Note that nothing happens on the meter that would indicate an electric current.

3. Now make Faraday's discovery. Move the magnet quickly in and out of the coil. Does the meter indicate a current?

4. Does the rate at which you move the magnet in and out of the coil affect the size of the current?

5. Have your partner hold the magnet while you move the coil back and forth over the magnet. Does it matter which moves, the coil or the magnet?

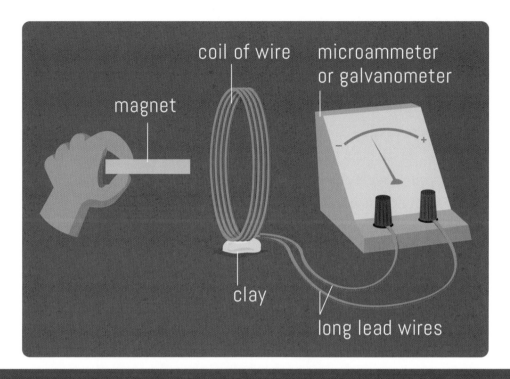

coil of wire   microammeter or galvanometer

magnet

clay

long lead wires

Figure 26. An electric current can be obtained by changing the magnetic field inside a coil of wire.

As you and Faraday discovered, it's not enough to have a magnetic field inside a coil of wire. The magnetic field must be changing. It's the changing magnetic field that is needed to generate electricity.

GLOSSARY

acceleration—the rate of change of velocity.

Ampère's rule—If your right thumb points in the direction of the electric current (positive charge flow) along a wire, your fingers curl in the direction of the magnetic field around the wire. (See Figure 25c.)

calorie—A unit of heat energy. 1 Calorie = 4.186 joules.

convex lens—A lens with at least one surface that curves outward. When parallel rays of light pass through a convex lens the refracted rays converge at one point.

kinetic energy—The energy a body has due to its motion.

light waves—Any and all waves in the electromagnetic spectrum including visible light, infrared, and radio waves made of oscillating magnetic and electrical fields.

momentum—The measure of the quantity of motion in a body. A product of mass and velocity.

parallel circuit—A closed circuit where the current divides into multiple paths before recombining to complete the circuit.

real image—Any image that can be projected on a screen.

reflection—The throwing back of a wave without it being absorbed.

refraction—The bending of light when it travels from one medium to another.

series circuit—A closed circuit in which the current follows a single path.

sound waves—A wave formed when a sound is created that then moves through an elastic medium such as air.

vectors—A quantity that has both direction and magnitude.

velocity—Distance travelled in a particular direction per unit of time.

virtual image—An image that is formed when reflected or refracted light rays appear to meet. Virtual images cannot be projected onto a screen.

work—Work occurs when a force acting on a body displaces that body. Work = force × distance.

FURTHER READING

BOOKS

Alley, Michael. *The Craft of Scientific Presentations: Critical Steps to Succeed and Critical Errors to Avoid.* New York: Springer Publishing, 2013.

Buczynski, Sandy. *Designing a Winning Science Fair Project.* Ann Arbor, MI: Cherry Lake Publishing, 2014.

Butterworth, Jon. *Most Wanted Particle: The Inside Story of the Hunt for Higgs, the Heart of the Future of Physics.* New York: The Experiment, 2015.

Curran, Greg. *Homework Helpers: Physcics, Revised Edition.* Dulles, VA: Career Press, 2012.

Franceschetti, Donald R. *Careers in Physics.* Hackensack, NJ: Salem Press. 2013.

Gardner, Robert. *The Physics of Sports Science Projects.* Berkeley Heights, NJ: Enslow Publishers, Inc., 2013.

Mercer, Bobby. *Junk Drawer Physics: 50 Awesome Experiments That Don't Cost a Thing.* Chicago: Chicago Review Press, Inc., 2014.

Reich, Samuel Eugene. *Plastic Fantasic: How the Biggest Fraud in Physics Shook the Scientific World.* New York: St. Martin's Griffin, 2010.

Trigg, George. *Landmark Experiments in Twentieth Century Physics.* Mineola, NY: Dover Publications, 2011.

WEBSITES

CERN Scientific Information Service
library.web.cern.ch/particle_physics_information
Lots of links for information on particle physics.

Harvard University
physics.harvard.edu/library/resources
A wide array of physics links.

Master's in Data Science
mastersindatascience.org/blog/the-ultimate-stem-guide-for-kids-239-cool-sites-about-science-technology-engineering-and-math/
Over 200 STEM links including challenges and contests.

MIT Open Courseware
ocw.mit.edu/high-school/
MIT's open resources for high school students interested in physics along with other sciences.

Science Reference Services
loc.gov/rr/scitech/selected-internet/physics.html
Links for physics societies, labs, and databases.

CAREER INFORMATION

APS Physics
aps.org/careers/
The American Physical Society's page on careers.

Big Future
bigfuture.collegeboard.org/majors-careers
A career and job based website with a focus on
college majors.

Physics.org
physics.org
A wealth of information including some great links
on careers.

Salary.com
swz.salary.com/SalaryWizard/Physicist-III-Job-Description.aspx
Salary expectations for a physicist with links and job
descriptions.

Science Pioneers
sciencepioneers.org/students/stem-websites
Links to various STEM career websites.

Society of Physics Students
spsnational.org
A community for physics students.

INDEX